A Contemporary Perspective on
LMS Railway Signalling
VOL 1

A Contemporary Perspective on
LMS Railway Signalling
VOL 1
Semaphore Swansong

Allen Jackson

THE CROWOOD PRESS

First published in 2015 by
The Crowood Press Ltd
Ramsbury, Marlborough
Wiltshire SN8 2HR

www.crowood.com

British Library Cataloguing-in-Publication Data
A catalogue record for this book is available from the British Library.

ISBN 978 1 78500 025 6

Dedication
For Ninette.

Acknowledgements
The kindness and interest shown by railway signallers.

Frontispiece: Blackpool North No. 2 signal box
with some of its signals, March 2010.

Typeset by Bookcraft Ltd, Stroud, Gloucestershire
Printed and bound in Malaysia by Times Offset (M) Sdn Bhd

Contents

Preface   6

Introduction   7

1   Signal Boxes and Infrastructure on Network Rail   8

2   Midland Railway   12
     Nottingham to Lincoln   12
     Settle to Carlisle   23
     Manchester to Sheffield   37
     Peterborough to Syston   48
     Worksop to Nottingham   58
     Burton upon Trent to Leicester   65
     Cheltenham Spa Area   68
     Chinley Junction to Buxton   70
     Leeds to Sheffield   75

3   Lancashire and Yorkshire Railway   78
     West Lancashire   79
     Walton Junction to Preston   85
     Wigan Wallgate to Kirkby   86
     North of Bolton   87
     Manchester to Oldham   88
     Manchester to Bradford   99
     Preston to Blackpool North   109
     North and East Lancashire   118
     West Yorkshire   124

4   Furness Railway   128

5   Glasgow and South Western Railway   150
     Ayr to Stranraer Harbour   150
     Carlisle to Glasgow   160

6   North Staffordshire Railway   175
     Stoke-on-Trent to Derby   176

Useful Resources   188

Index   189

Preface

The GWR book in this series concentrated more on the ways of working, and while it would be easy and more lucrative to refer readers back to that volume, some explanations of those features have been incorporated in this work. I apologize if this seems slightly repetitive if you have already read the GWR book but I feel there will be some who have not.

Fig. 1   Forest of semaphore signals at Blackpool North station, August 2005.

Introduction

Up until 1 January 1923 there were hundreds of railway companies in Britain. The government at the time perceived an administrative difficulty in controlling the railways' activities at times of national crisis. The country had just endured World War I and the feeling was that it could all be managed better if they were amalgamated. Thus came the railway 'grouping', as it was termed, creating just four railway companies.

The London Midland and Scottish Railway was one of those four entities but the identities of the larger companies within it persisted and do so to this day. Lines are referred to by their pre-grouping ownership even now. This is often because routes were duplicated and so it was never going to be accurate to refer to the line from 'Manchester to Sheffield' without the qualification 'Midland Railway' if that was the one being referred to. This was to differentiate between the lines run by the Great Central.

Many of the smaller companies did lose their identity, in signalling terms, although their architecture may remain.

The only pre-grouping railways considered therefore are those for which an identifiable signalling presence existed at the time of the survey.

The ex-LMS signal boxes and infrastructure amount to 244 examples, so it has been necessary to split the LMS into two.

Volume 1 covers:

- Midland Railway (MR)
- Lancashire and Yorkshire Railway (L&YR)
- Furness Railway (FR)
- Glasgow and South Western Railway (GSWR)
- North Staffordshire Railway (NSR)

Volume 2 covers:

- London and North Western Railway (LNWR)
- Caledonian Railway (CR)
- Highland Railway (HR)

In the book the system of units used is the imperial system, which is what the railways themselves still use, although there has been a move to introduce metric units in places like the Railway Accident Investigation Branch reports and in the southeast of England, where there are connections to the Channel Tunnel.

As a guide:

- 1 mile = 1.6km
- 1 yard = 0.92m
- 1 chain = 20.11m
- 1 chain = 22 yards
- 1 mile = 1,760 yards or 80 chains.

CHAPTER I

Signal Boxes and Infrastructure on Network Rail

The survey was carried out between 2003 and 2014 and represents a wide cross-section of the remaining signal boxes on Network Rail. Inevitably some have closed and been demolished, while others have been preserved and moved away.

Although the book is organized around the pre-grouping companies, the passage of time has meant that some pre-grouping structures have been replaced by LMS or BR buildings.

If you are intending visiting any of them it is suggested that you find out what the current status is before you set off.

For reasons of access and position some signal boxes are covered in greater detail than others and some are featured as a 'focus on' where the quality of the information or the interest of that location merits that attention.

Some of the signal boxes have been reduced in status over the years and while they may have controlled block sections in the past some no longer do so, but are (or were at the time of the survey) on Network Rail's payroll as working signal boxes.

Details of the numbers of levers are included but not all the levers may be fully functional as signal boxes have been constantly modified over the years.

Lever colours are:

Red	Home signals
Yellow	Distant signals
Black	Points
Blue	Facing-point locks
Blue/brown	Wicket gates at level crossings
Black/Yellow chevrons	Detonator placers
White	Not in use
Green	King lever to cancel locking when box switched out.

Levers under the block shelf, or towards the front window normally, are said to be normal and those pulled over to the rear of the box are said to be reversed.

There are some boxes where the levers are mounted the opposite way round, in other words levers in the normal position point to the rear wall, but the convention remains the same.

Listed Buildings

Many signal boxes are considered to have architectural or historic merit and are Grade II listed by English Heritage or Historic Scotland. This basically means they cannot be changed externally without permission. If the owner allows the building to decay to such an extent that it is unsafe, the building can then be demolished. The number of signal boxes with a listing is due to increase following the news that they are all to be replaced by 2020.

There are currently sixty-four boxes across the network that are under consideration for listing, so whilst the listing status is given as being accurate when this was written, the status may well change. A Grade I listing would require the interiors to remain the same so that is unlikely to happen with Network Rail structures but may happen with the preservation movement – many boxes have had the interiors preserved as fully operational working museums.

In Scotland the classification system is somewhat different and is as follows: Category A for buildings of national or international architectural worth or intrinsic merit; Category B for buildings of regional architectural worth or intrinsic merit; Category C for buildings of local importance, architectural worth or intrinsic merit.

Signal Box Official Abbreviation

Most signal boxes on Network Rail have an official abbreviation of one, two or sometimes three letters. This usually appears on all signal posts relevant to that box. Finding an abbreviation could be tricky – for example there are eight signal boxes with Norton in the title – until you realize that they are not unique. The abbreviation for each box appears after the box title in this book, if it has one.

Ways of Working

Absolute Block – AB

A concept used almost since railways began is the 'block' of track where a train is permitted to move from block to block provided no other train was in the block being moved to. This relies on there being up and down tracks. Single lines have their own arrangements. It is usual to consider trains travelling towards London to be heading in the up direction, but there are local variations.

This block system was worked by block instruments that conveyed the track occupancy status and by a bell system that was used to communicate with adjacent signal boxes.

Track Circuit Block – TCB

Track circuit block is really all to do with colour light signals, which, strictly speaking are outside the scope of this book, except that many signal boxes interface to track circuit block sections and will have track circuit block equipment or indications in them.

Originally track circuits lit a lamp in a signal box to indicate where a train was. Then they were used to interlock block instruments, signals and points together to provide a safe working semaphore signal environment.

With colour light signals it is possible to provide automatically changing signals that are controlled by the passage of trains or presence of vehicles on the track.

Single Line Workings

These – key token, tokenless block and no signaller key token – are covered in detail in the section on the signal box that supervises such workings.

The suffix [i] behind a box title indicates interior views.

Summary of Disposition LMS Volume I

Midland Railway

Nottingham to Lincoln
- Lowdham
- Fiskerton Junction
- Fiskerton Station
- Rolleston Crossing
- Staythorpe Crossing
- Newark Castle
- Swinderby

Settle to Carlisle
- Hellifield South Junction
- Settle Junction
- Blea Moor
- Garsdale (Hawes Junction)
- Kirkby Stephen
- Appleby North
- Kirkby Thore
- Culgaith
- Low House Crossing
- Howe and Co.'s Siding

Manchester to Sheffield
- Romiley Junction
- New Mills Central
- New Mills South Junction
- Chinley Junction
- Edale
- Earle's Sidings
- Grindleford
- Totley Tunnel East

Peterborough to Syston
- Uffington and Barnack
- Stamford Station
- Ketton
- Manton Junction
- Oakham Level Crossing
- Langham Junction
- Ashwell
- Whissendine
- Melton Mowbray Station

Worksop to Nottingham
- Elmton and Creswell
- Shirebrook Junction
- Pinxton
- Sleight's Sidings East
- Stanton Gate Shunt Frame
- Stapleford and Sandiacre
- Sneinton Crossing Shunt Frame

Burton upon Trent to Leicester
- Bardon Hill
- Mantle Lane
- Moira West Junction

Cheltenham Spa Area
- Alstone Crossing
- Oddingley

Chinley Junction to Buxton
- Peak Forest South
- Great Rocks Junction

Leeds to Sheffield
- Moorthorpe
- Hickleton

Lancashire and Yorkshire Railway

West Lancashire
- Burscough Bridge Junction
- Parbold
- Wigan Wallgate
- Crow Nest Junction
- Atherton Goods Yard
- Walkden

Walton Junction to Preston
- Rufford
- Midge Hall

Wigan Wallgate to Kirkby
- Rainford Junction

North of Bolton
- Blackrod Junction
- Bromley Cross

Manchester to Oldham
- Ashton Moss North Junction
- Baguley Fold Junction
- Vitriol Works
- Castleton East Junction
- Rochdale
- Shaw Station
- Oldham Mumps

Manchester to Bradford
- Smithy Bridge
- Hebden Bridge
- Milner Royd Junction [i]
- Halifax
- Mill Lane Junction
- Greetland
- Elland [i]

Preston to Blackpool North
- Salwick
- Kirkham
- Poulton-le-Fylde (No. 3)
- Carleton Crossing
- Blackpool North No. 1
- Blackpool North No. 2

North and East Lancashire
- Bamber Bridge Level Crossing Frame (LCF)
- Huncoat LCF
- Towneley LCF
- Daisyfield Station
- Horrocksford Junction
- Brierfield Station

West Yorkshire
- Cutsyke Junction
- Prince of Wales Colliery
- Hensall

Furness Railway

- Carnforth Station Junction
- Arnside
- Grange-over-Sands
- Ulverston
- Dalton Junction [i]
- Barrow-in-Furness
- Park South [i]
- Askam
- Foxfield
- Millom
- Silecroft
- Bootle
- Drigg
- Sellafield
- St Bees

Glasgow and South Western Railway

Ayr to Stranraer Harbour

- Kilkerran [i]
- Girvan
- Barrhill [i]
- Glenwhilly
- Dunragit
- Stranraer Harbour

Carlisle to Glasgow

- Annan
- Dumfries Station
- Holywood
- Thornhill
- Kirkconnel
- New Cumnock
- Mauchline
- Hurlford
- Lugton [i]

North Staffordshire Railway

Stoke-on-Trent to Derby

- Foley Crossing
- Caverswall
- Uttoxeter
- Sudbury
- Scropton [i]
- Tutbury Crossing
- Egginton Junction [i]

This does not claim to be an all-encompassing list and there are odd stragglers that were not surveyed and are now no more.

Fig. 2   Peak Forest South in Derbyshire, October 2014.

CHAPTER 2

Midland Railway

The Midland Railway was one of the earliest of the larger railway companies and, like so many others, its wealth was built on the movement of coal.

The Midland Railway was often held up in the nineteenth century as being a sure-fire investment. It was returning 6.5 per cent as a dividend when the bank rate was averaging about half that.

The Midland expanded wherever it could into South Wales, the south coast of England with the Somerset and Dorset Joint Railway (S&DJR) and eventually towards Scotland with the Settle and Carlisle line. It was in the Midlands coalfields where the company made its money. The main line ran from St Pancras in London to Leicester, Sheffield, Leeds and Carlisle. It also had a passenger presence from Bristol to Birmingham and access to the Somerset coalfield through the S&DJR. The company's centre was at Derby, where the first ever roundhouse, for Derby Locomotive Works, was built in 1839 and is now an exhibition centre and listed building. The Midland developed a strong rivalry with, mostly, the London and North Western Railway. Derby has remained a centre of technical excellence on the railways and an influence in railway matters generally, where it has been seen to 'get its way' much to the annoyance of other railway company proponents.

The Midland Railway was also a 50 per cent shareholder in the Cheshire Lines Committee (CLC) but as this is seen as a predominantly London and North Eastern Railway concern, despite most of it being in Lancashire, it has been held over for one of the LNER volumes in this series.

Nottingham to Lincoln

The area from Nottingham to Lincoln is one of contrasts. Nottingham was for many years the world's centre of lace-making and many innovative techniques were pioneered in the city. It was surrounded by coalfields, and Toton Yard was a massive coal train marshalling complex.

Tobacco and light industries featured in the city's portfolio of activities with the world-famous Raleigh cycle factory. These works had their heyday when a good proportion of the working population in the 1950s used a cycle to get to work.

Lincolnshire is often considered a flat county of farmland but has delightful undulating scenery around Horncastle and Market Rasen in the Lincolnshire Wolds area.

Lincoln itself was originally built on a hill. The hill was named Lindum by the Romans, who were its founders. Lincoln, as well as being an administrative centre for the county and surrounding agricultural area, was also a manufacturer of small locomotives for industrial use and farm machinery.

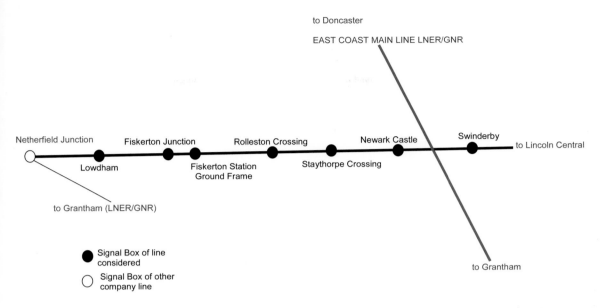

Fig. 3   Nottingham–Lincoln schematic diagram.

The Midland Railway ran into their own station at St Marks in the city centre and added to the bane of pedestrians' and road vehicle drivers' lives – the street level crossing.

The schematic not-to-scale diagram in Fig. 3 shows only mechanical signal boxes. The journey will be from east to west.

Lowdham (LH)

Date Built	1896
MR Type or Builder	MR Type 2b
No. of Levers	16
Ways of Working	AB
Current Status	Active
Listed (Y/N)	N

Lowdham is a prosperous and pretty village on the road to Southwell, that minster cathedral in rurality. Lowdham rated a mention in the Domesday Book and part of St Mary's church dates from medieval days. The village was much occupied with frame knitting in the nineteenth century.

Lowdham station and signal box are examples of typical Midland Railway architecture and ambience. The signal box depicted in Fig. 4 is the archetypical 'Airfix kit' design although the steps are now galvanized steel.

The Airfix kit refers to a manufacturer of plastic OO gauge model railway kits in the 1950s and 1960s, and the signal box was actually modelled on Oakham, which appears later in the book. The only features missing are the platform walkway and railings at first-floor level.

Fig. 4   Lowdham signal box, May 2006.

Fig. 5   Lowdham goods yard crossing and single slip, May 2006.

Lowdham signal box is 7 miles and 27 chains (11.8km) from Nottingham East Junction near Nottingham Midland station.

Fig. 5 shows an unusual manifestation of a feature once so common. Most railway companies had a fear of placing points so that their blades faced the normal running direction because the force of a train hitting facing points can, under certain circumstances, force the point blades to open and cause a derailment. The right-hand line running direction is towards the camera, and to gain access to the now long closed goods yard it was necessary to travel past the point in the foreground and reverse across the diamond crossing and into the yard, thereby avoiding a running line facing point situation. The siding and its crossover have been retained for engineers' use. Note the angled paling fencing – this is typical of the Midland Railway but is obviously a much later replacement. The view is towards Newark and Lincoln.

Fig. 6 shows the arrow-straight line towards Nottingham with just a glimpse of the starter signal behind the box and beyond the road overbridge. The platform edge has been refaced with concrete slabs although some of the original paving exists further down the platform.

The splendid Midland station building survives in private hands and the owner has sympathetically retained a lot of the original character. The building would have doubled as a stationmaster's residence as well as a booking office, parcels office

Fig. 6   Lowdham looking towards Nottingham, May 2006.

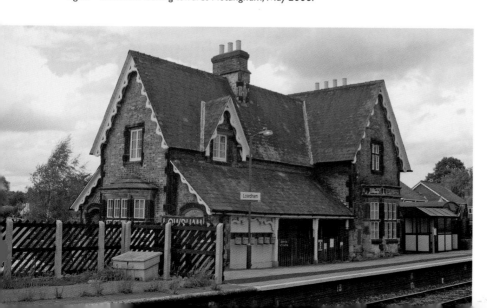

Fig. 7   Lowdham station building, May 2006.

and waiting room for passengers. Fig. 7 shows this to advantage.

Period features to note are the scalloped barge boards, blue enamel name board, fire buckets and postbox. Note also the difference in ancient and modern platform edging. The Network Rail bus shelter is in attendance. The ventilated goods van body looks as though it is in use as a wood store.

Fiskerton Junction (FJ)

Date Built	1929
MR Type or Builder	MR Type 4e
No. of Levers	30
Ways of Working	AB
Current Status	Active
Listed (Y/N)	N

As with so many of the signal boxes termed junction, there is no longer a junction here. The box was built in 1929 to control a line put in to service two collieries that had opened up in the 1920s, just before the Depression. The collieries closed but the line stayed there until 1966; during the interim the collieries had reopened and outlived the railway that had been built for them.

The box in Fig. 8 is in good condition with replacement uPVC windows and steel steps to replace the wooden ones, though there are no roof finials. Unlike other boxes in other regions, the Midland boxes have not generally had toilet blocks grafted on but seem to have a separate building or Portaloo. The box worked its gates from a mechanical wheel within the box at the time of the survey. The box is 12 miles 3 chains (19.4km) from Nottingham East Junction.

Fig. 9 shows the single trailing crossover that the box controls together with inner home and distant signals. The distant signal is Fiskerton Station's as the distance between the two boxes is short, at about half a mile (800m). The ground signal on the left is to signal a reversing move over the trailing crossover.

Fig. 10 is an image of the rear of Fiskerton Junction signal box. The wooden-framed structure

Fig. 8   Fiskerton Junction signal box, May 2006.

Fig. 9   Fiskerton Junction's home signal on the same post as Fiskerton Station signal box's distant signal, May 2006.

Fig. 10   Rear of Fiskerton Junction signal box, May 2006.

Fig. 11   Morton Crossing ground frame, May 2006.

at the end appears to be some sort of bird feeder. The crossing keeper's cottage over the tracks has acquired a new gentility, with a brick toilet block at the end.

Back up the line a short way towards Nottingham, the Morton Crossing ground frame is shown in Fig. 11. This is what was here before the signal box was built in 1929 and has somehow survived. It controlled the crossing and signals. There is a lever within Fiskerton Junction signal box to release control of the crossing to the ground frame.

Fiskerton Station

Date Built	1902
MR Type or Builder	MR Type 3a
No. of Levers	16
Ways of Working	Gate
Current Status	Active
Listed (Y/N)	N

Fiskerton lies on the bank of the River Trent and has many large homes belonging to wealthy

Fig. 12   Fiskerton Station signal box, May 2006.

Fig. 13   Rear of Fiskerton Station signal box, May 2006.

businesspeople who used the station to commute to Nottingham. Fiskerton rated a mention in the Domesday Book and became industrialized to some extent as the river was a main trade artery. After the arrival of the railway in 1846 the riverside industries fell into disuse and the village became gentrified.

There is a two-platform station with the usual bus shelters but the original station building survives in private hands. The station is 12 miles and 46 chains (20.4km) from Nottingham East Junction.

Fig. 12 depicts the box in rural splendour. The signaller has gone to some trouble to brighten up the working environment with a fine display of window boxes and planter tubs – there is even a trellis against the toilet wall.

This is not a block post in the sense that trains have to be passed from one block to another as in the case of absolute block (AB); so, as it only looks after a crossing, it gains the soubriquet 'Gate'.

The conifer in the barrel tub in the rear of Fiskerton Station signal box must be part of the winter garden display and is taking a back seat to the May blossom on display in Fig. 13. The trellis appears to have young clematis growing. If you like nature this is a good place to work – or rather, the signaller has made it so.

The view is towards Nottingham.

Fig. 14 gives a glimpse inside the box at Fiskerton Station. The two levers pulled off are a home and distant signal. The distant signals on this line are remarkable semaphore survivors when, even in predominantly semaphore areas, colour light distants are almost universally used. Colour lights are much better in fog and low-light conditions. The lever frame is a typical Midland Railway type that was subsequently adopted by the LMS. All points and signals are interlocked to prevent an unsafe movement from being signalled, and the frame contains some of the levers and other devices to do this.

The Midland locking frame was extraordinarily compact and this meant the box did not need to be very high just to accommodate the locking in a special room underneath the frame. The London

Fig. 14   Fiskerton Station signal box lever frame with home and distant signals pulled off, May 2006.

Fig. 15   Fiskerton Station inner home and distant in the Nottingham direction, May 2006.

Fig. 16   Rolleston Crossing signal box, May 2006.

Fig. 17   Rolleston station and MR wooden post signal, May 2006.

and North Western Railway was said to have been the opposite in this respect.

It was not always geographically convenient to have the points and signals interlocked at the frame and where this happens outside the box it is referred to as 'slotting' or 'detection'.

Finally at Fiskerton Station, Fig. 15 shows the inner home and distant signals for the Nottingham (up) direction. They both have sighting boards that eliminate a confusing visual background to the eyes of the driver. The distant signal is controlled by Fiskerton Junction signal box as the two locations are so close to one another.

Rolleston Crossing

Date Built	c.1980
MR Type or Builder	BR Portakabin
No. of Levers	–
Ways of Working	Gate
Current Status	Active, closure slated
Listed (Y/N)	N

Rolleston has the standard two platform and bus shelter arrangement and sees traffic for Southwell racecourse.

The box is just that – a box – in Fig. 16, and is about as basic as a signal box gets. It does not have the saving grace of architectural merit, and unsurprisingly there has been no clamour to list it.

Fiskerton's up distant signal, towards Nottingham, at Rolleston station (Fig. 17), on the other hand, is a Midland Railway survivor complete with wooden post, although the arm is a standard LMS upper quadrant as opposed to Midland lower quadrant. Wooden post signals are now rare on Network Rail.

Staythorpe Crossing (SK)

Date Built	c.1950
MR Type or Builder	LMS Type 11c
No. of Levers	35
Ways of Working	AB
Current Status	Active
Listed (Y/N)	N

Fig. 18   Staythorpe Crossing signal box, May 2006.

Fig. 19   Staythorpe Crossing signal box and the siding to the former power stations, May 2006.

Now we come to the first ex-LMS box on this line and the build date tells us that the London Midland Region of British Railways used an LMS box that had been stored at Crewe during World War II as a replacement for bomb-damaged signal boxes. Some were stored at Crewe Works in kit form for just such an eventuality. There doesn't appear to have been a Plan B if Crewe Works had been bombed, but perhaps there were other storage locations.

The box was built not only as a block post on the line but to supervise the junction with a power station also named Staythorpe (and later Staythorpe A).

It was extended by six feet in 1960 to look after the sidings put in for Staythorpe B power station. This is clearly visible at the far end in Fig. 18, as is the sag in the middle. Perhaps there is such a thing as signal box botox.

The barriers are operated from a panel within the box.

Both power stations, A and B, were closed – in 1983 and 1994 respectively – and a new (2010) gas-fired power station occupies the site.

Fig. 19 is looking towards Newark and Lincoln at Staythorpe Crossing signal box, and the siding to one of the power stations is still there at the survey date. Note that the point that gives access to the power station is facing, and that T-shaped piece between the track and the point blades is a facing-point lock mechanism. This requires a separate blue lever in the signal box.

The high-voltage distribution power lines are visible; although at the time of the survey no power was being generated, that infrastructure remained.

Staythorpe Crossing signal box is 14 miles 20 chains (23km) from Nottingham East Junction.

Fig. 20   Staythorpe Crossing signal box and the signals to the former power stations, May 2006.

Fig. 21   Rear of Staythorpe Crossing signal box, May 2006.

The yellow quarter-mile post on the right of the picture bears this out as 20 chains is one quarter of a mile. The full-mile distance is usually on the top of the post, and you add both values to get the true mileage.

Fig. 20 looks the other way towards Nottingham, and the bracket signal subsidiary posts are to control entry to the power station sidings. The main post is straight on for Newark. The trailing crossover is signalled by the ground discs to permit reversing moves. Note the guy wires to steady the signal post.

Fig. 21 shows the rear of Staythorpe Crossing signal box with cranked staircase to keep clear of

the road. Note that the white gate dates from an earlier period than the paling fence, which is distinctly non-Midland Railway in character.

Newark Castle (NC)

Date Built	1912
MR Type or Builder	MR Type 4a
No. of Levers	16
Ways of Working	AB, TCB
Current Status	Active
Listed (Y/N)	N

Newark, on the bank of the River Trent, has its origins in Roman times as it was a stopping point on the Fosse Way. Newark Castle is now a ruin and the skirmishes in the English Civil War can't have helped. However, the town grew as a marketplace and a centre for the textile trades. Nowadays it is handily placed for commuters to London and Nottingham and is a prosperous growing town that retains a good deal of character.

Newark itself is more properly named Newark-on-Trent, and the station Newark Castle has been termed thus to distinguish it from the ex-London and North Eastern Railway station, Newark North Gate, on the East Coast Main Line.

This is one of the few places in Britain where a main line is crossed by another main line on the flat with rail crossings.

Fig. 22   Newark Castle signal box, May 2006.

Fig. 23   Newark Castle station, former MR building, May 2006.

There are only ground semaphore signals here and a crossover. Newark Castle works AB to Staythorpe Crossing signal box and TCB to Doncaster power box. Newark Castle signal box is 16 miles 79 chains (27.3km) from Nottingham East Junction and lies at the Nottingham end of the down platform, as shown in Fig. 22; the view is back along the line to Staythorpe Crossing. This box has its frame in the rear – in other words the levers point to the rear of the box when in their normal position.

Fig. 23 shows some fine Midland architecture in the generous station building. This is looking back towards Lincoln and from the same point as Fig. 22. The building on the far left under the '2' is the former goods shed, which has now been converted for private business use.

Fig. 24 shows the trailing crossover and ground disc signals, which account for only three levers in the frame. The crossover is used as some trains from Nottingham terminate here. The train arrives on the down platform on the left and reverses over the crossover to begin another journey back to Nottingham.

The former goods shed can be seen with the iron struts for the awning still in place; the archway where the wagons would go in now has a large multi-panelled window in the aperture there. There were goods sidings on both sides together with an interchange siding with the Great Northern Railway as well as a short branch line to a sugar beet factory.

Fig. 24   Newark Castle station, goods shed and crossover, May 2006.

Fig. 25   Swinderby signal box, February 2007.

Swinderby (SY)

Date Built	1901
MR Type or Builder	MR Type 3a
No. of Levers	16
Ways of Working	TCB
Current Status	Active
Listed (Y/N)	N

Swinderby is east of the East Coast Main Line and the first station on the Nottingham to Lincoln line in Lincolnshire. Swinderby was the home of a World War II bomber base, one of many in Lincolnshire, and was notable for the number of Polish squadrons based there who fought for Britain. In 1964 it became a recruit training base until RAF Swinderby closed in 1993 and the site was redeveloped.

Fig. 25 shows a well-kept and looked-after box. The replacement windows are a little on the chunky side but perhaps that is because they are double glazed. There is a neat brick-built toilet block. It is unusual for a box this small to have a walkway and railings around it.

In the view down towards Lincoln shown in Fig. 26, the ballast pile is the site of the former goods yard. Note the period 50mph speed restriction sign on the up right-hand side. The point

Fig. 26   Swinderby signal box looking towards Lincoln, February 2007.

Fig. 27   Swinderby signal box looking towards Nottingham, February 2007.

rodding coming out of the box is on its own, as a crossover only needs one rod and lever to make it work. The points in a crossover are co-acting and so the rodding and cranks are arranged to make both points operate with one black lever pull. If the crossover is facing the normal direction of traffic, it needs a blue lever to release both locks first before a crossover can be changed. Power-operated points don't usually need a facing-point lock lever as the locking is integral with the mechanism.

The view in Fig. 27 is looking up the line towards Newark and Nottingham. The home signal on the right is much taller than its partner on the left as the line undulates after the station and the taller signal is needed to be seen. Note the 'W' whistle roundel which is modern and odd in that trains no longer whistle but either hoot or bray. On the left-hand side is a period waiting shelter.

Fig. 28   Swinderby station building and stationmaster's house, February 2007.

Fig. 29   Rear view of Swinderby signal box, February 2007.

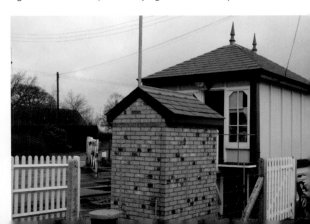

Fig. 30   Swinderby station parcels depot, February 2007.

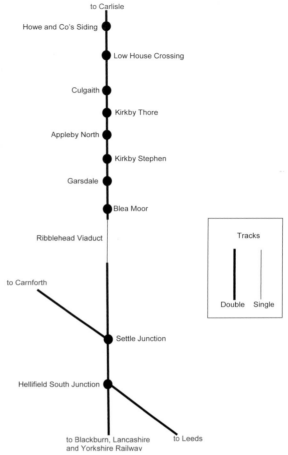

Fig. 31   Settle–Carlisle Line schematic diagram.

The delightful station building and stationmaster's house (now in private care) are shown in Fig. 28. Stationmasters had no choice but to live 'on the job' so to speak but this would appear to be no hardship at Swinderby. Stations would go to some lengths to cultivate gardens for the passengers and competitions would be held and prizes awarded for excellence. There would often be some railway land nearby that was cultivated for vegetables as with an allotment, and sometimes vegetables changed hands for a large lump of coal from the tender or bunker. If coal was hard to come by there would usually be a supply of old sleepers that had been creosoted and would burn well when split. Old sleepers often manifested themselves as garden sheds or pigsties.

Swinderby station is 24 miles and 64 chains (40km) from Nottingham East Junction.

Fig. 29 is a view of Swinderby box from the rear. It is unusual in that this crossing box has no rearward-facing windows.

From here the line and mileages change as the trains run onto Great Northern railway metals and into Lincoln Central. St Marks station together with its Midland Railway box closed in 1985.

Fig. 30 is the waiting shelter on the up side and what appears to have been a parcels office where items would be lodged whilst waiting for a train.

Settle to Carlisle

The Midland Railway never seemed to be concerned with physical obstacles when building the railway: they would just as soon go over as go around. They also pursued a policy of using smaller engines than other companies and if that meant a lot of trains had to be banked or assisted over steep gradients then so be it. Both these policies were to be taxed to the limit when the Midland Railway board decided that they would like a piece of the Scottish market. Their bitter rivals the London and

North Western Railway held sway in the north-west of England and effectively blocked a Midland Railway train from going to Scotland by the routes that were there then.

Midland Railway's most northerly railhead of any size up until then was Leeds, and from there they decided to cross or straddle the Pennine mountain chain along the backbone of England to make a junction eventually at Carlisle. Midland Railway engines would make way for Glasgow and South Western Railway ones at Carlisle for the trip to Glasgow St Enoch's station. Glasgow was, at that time, Britain's second largest city. In BR days trains also ran over the S&C to Edinburgh by the Waverley route, which is just being relaid with track after having been ripped up in 1969.

The Midland Railway's 'go over' policy had to be modified to do this, and while there are steep gradients there are also fifteen tunnels and many viaducts in the 73 miles (117km) from Settle to Carlisle. The human cost in building the railway was heavy and there are graves to this day in local churchyards commemorating those who died during the construction.

Of the viaducts, by far the most famous and the longest is Ribblehead. It was repairs to this structure, according to British Rail, that nearly precipitated the closure of the whole line. The BR tactics of closure by stealth met with opposition from the Friends of the Settle–Carlisle Line and a successful campaign was mounted that culminated in the Minister for Transport, Michael Portillo, abandoning closure and/or selling-off plans in 1989. Time has proved that this was a far-sighted and wise move and the line now sees healthy passenger numbers as well as mass freight traffic that use the S&C in preference to the West Coast Main Line, which would struggle to provide paths for any more freight than it currently can accommodate.

Hellifield South Junction has been added to the Settle–Carlisle Line, although it is not generally regarded as being part of it, as it helps to show the overall picture and it would be an orphan if left out of the S&C story.

Partly as a result of the controversies of the 1980s and concern about its serviceability, Ribblehead viaduct was reduced to single-track working. In addition, many of the block sections of the line are divided up into two to permit more traffic on the line.

The block section allows one train into the block at a time. When an intermediate block section (IBS) is introduced into a block, this splits the block into two and thereby theoretically doubles the number of trains that can be worked. The S&C is also used as a diversionary route when the West Coast Main Line is closed.

The electric trains are usually pulled over the route by a class 57 diesel.

Hellifield South Junction (H)

Date Built	1911
MR Type or Builder	MR Type 4c
No. of Levers	58
Ways of Working	AB
Current Status	Active
Listed (Y/N)	N

Hellifield station is somewhat isolated and yet is still an important railway junction; indeed events over the past thirty years have brought that importance

Fig. 32   Hellifield South Junction signal box, March 2007.

into sharp focus. It is all the better that the place is looked after and cared for.

The Midland Railway did not skimp on the building and facilities here, and as well as a fine passenger station there were extensive goods yards, three signal boxes and an engine shed.

Hellifield was also the scene of a railway accident in 1955. An express train from St Pancras to Edinburgh was held at the platform at Hellifield with a defective brake on a sleeping car whilst fitters tried to fix it. As a result of bad signalling design a following express ran into the back of the Edinburgh-bound train at an estimated 30mph (50km/h). No one was even badly injured, not even the carriage fitter, who had been lying on the track trying to fix the faulty brake on the sleeping car. The signaller was hauled over the coals.

Fig. 32 shows an impressive-looking box that has had its lever count reduced to fifty-eight over the years from the original sixty-four. The line that has the bracket signal is the line from Skipton and Leeds, and it is electrified on the overhead 25kV system as far as Skipton. The line curving away to the right is the Lancashire and Yorkshire Railway line to Blackburn. Hellifield South Junction is 231 miles 14 chains (372km) from St Pancras station via Nottingham and Leeds.

Fig. 33 is looking up the down main – the down direction is towards Carlisle but the camera is pointing back towards Leeds. As well as the down goods loop, there is a refuge siding beyond that leads to engineer's and two other sidings. The awning is a symphony in cast iron with the Midland Railway logo or initials picked out in black. There was a cheery café on the platform at the survey date. Note the difference in platform heights: the higher is where the trains stop now.

Still looking backwards to Leeds, Fig. 34 shows the other side of the station on the up platform. The gantry signals trains either straight on to Leeds,

Fig. 33   Hellifield station, March 2007.

Fig. 34   Hellifield station looking back towards Leeds, March 2007.

Fig. 35   Hellifield station looking towards Carlisle, March 2007.

Fig. 36   Hellifield station looking towards Carlisle, with a class 60 on an empty coal train, March 2007.

on the left, or to the Blackburn branch. Signal gantries are quite rare nowadays as they have been replaced by bracket signals wherever possible. This is the passenger side of the platform as opposed to the preserved side. Note there is Midland Railway-pattern replacement fencing.

Fig. 35 is looking down to Carlisle, and the demarcation between travelling passengers and the preserved part is more evident. There's more cast iron, although some designers got the drainpipes to run inside the columns – more aesthetically pleasing but an access problem. The sidings on the left

where the green shelter is are leased by the West Coast Railway Company, who run steam and diesel specials, some over the S&C. Their main base is at Carnforth, which will be covered in Chapter 4. West Coast is the owner of the steam loco Hogwarts Castle as used in the Harry Potter films to haul the Hogwarts Express and well known to GWR enthusiasts as 5972 Olton Hall. Other charter companies run steam and diesel specials over the S&C too.

The main freight commodities carried over the S&C are coal and gypsum with occasional cement trains. The class 60 in Fig. 36 is running back to Ayrshire in Scotland with coal empties. The disused platform bay with buffer stop is of period interest. There is a further bay on the up side. The locomotive depot in steam days was near the buffer stops on the far right-hand side. The depot was closed by BR in 1963 but it remained in use to store renovated exhibits for the National Railway Museum until the end of steam and the conversion of York North loco sheds into part of the NRM.

West Coast Railway's depot occupies some of Fig. 37 but of interest are the two siding starter signals: ancient and modern with modernized galvanised steel with health and safety hoops and platform together with a wooden post signal that is maybe eighty years old.

Fig. 37   Hellifield station looking towards Carlisle, West Coast Rail depot, March 2007.

Settle Junction (SJ)

Date Built	1913
MR Type or Builder	MR Type 4c
No. of Levers	31
Ways of Working	AB
Current Status	Active
Listed (Y/N)	N

Fig. 38   Settle Junction signal box, March 2007.

The approach to the Settle–Carlisle proper is at Settle Junction. The signal box is 232 miles 42 chains (374.2km) from St Pancras, and Settle station is still nearly 2 miles (3km) away.

Fig. 38 shows a box in splendid condition and subject to an award, judging by the blue plaque. The stovepipe is a hallmark of period presentation as coal stoves were done away with years ago. Wooden staircase and roof finials, together with sympathetically done replacement windows, complete the picture. There doesn't appear to be room for a toilet block outside the box so one is grafted on at first-floor level.

The junction to Carnforth is of the single-lead type, on the right in Fig. 39 and just after the trailing crossover. This means that although the two lines are double track, the actual junction is formed by one point that is then followed by another to revert to double track. While this is undoubtedly cheaper in maintenance terms than a double junction, it is not safer from an operational point of view and there have been accidents attributed to single-lead junctions. However, the line to Carnforth and Morecambe was not heavily used at the time of the survey.

The class 66 and coal empties are taking the S&C on the left and the bracket signal is pulled off for it. The other branch of the bracket is for the Carnforth line. There is another train due from the S&C from the next box along, which is Blea Moor – the signal on the far left gives the indication.

Fig. 39   Class 66 and an empty coal train take the Settle–Carlisle Line at Settle Junction, October 2014.

Fig. 40   Class 66 and its loaded coal train come off the Settle–Carlisle Line at Settle Junction, October 2014.

Fig. 41   Class 66 and coal train empties power up towards Settle station, with the Carnforth route on the left, October 2014.

The train signalled in Fig. 39 to come off the S&C to the junction to go towards Hellifield has arrived in Fig. 40. The loaded coal train with a class 66 has just come over Ais Gill summit pulling about 1,500 tons so may be forgiven for being a long time in the section.

The line from Settle Junction to Blea Moor signal box has intermediate block sections (IBS) on both up and down lines as far as Ribblehead viaduct, which is single track.

The Midland route to Carnforth is on the left. There was a signal box at Wennington Junction, about halfway to Carnforth, but the signaller was ill for a long time and the box was unstaffed in the meantime. Eventually the box was closed and the seemingly low traffic densities must have been a factor.

The Scots have a song about the low and high road: these roads don't go to the same place but the high road of the S&C, on the right, seems more inviting with the stunning scenery up ahead (Fig. 41). The class 66 and coal empties are doing about 60mph (100km/h) at this point and will make short work of it.

Blea Moor (BM)

Date Built	1941
MR Type or Builder	LMS Type 11c
No. of Levers	30
Ways of Working	AB
Current Status	Active
Listed (Y/N)	N

Perhaps Blea Moor should be renamed Bleak Moor in sympathy with Charles Dickens' novel – if ever a place was windswept and lonely, this is it.

The box pictured in Fig. 42, looking towards Carlisle, conveys just this aspect. There appears to be a guy wire attached to the box wall, presumably to stop the structure blowing away. The box is 247 miles 39 chains (398.3km) from St Pancras.

Fig. 42   Blea Moor signal box, November 2006.

In Fig. 43 the up goods loop is in front of the box and the double track is narrowing to become single to cross Ribblehead viaduct. The single-track section lasts for just over half a mile and then it resumes double track just before Ribblehead station. The point at Ribblehead station is operated by the Blea Moor signaller. There is a pair of sidings at Ribblehead station but they are operated by ground frame by locomotive crews. Typically the ground frame would be released by the Blea Moor signaller.

Fig. 44 is looking towards Carlisle, with the track going to single on the left; the up goods loop nearest the camera continues for a piece. The taller posted signal is for the goods loop and the shorter for the up line towards Leeds. The cottage on the right was still inhabited at the time of the survey, and after this is the Blea Moor tunnel, which runs for 1 mile and 869 yards (2.4km). The hill above it rises to 1,151ft (351m). From here to Garsdale there are no IBS.

Garsdale (G)

Date Built	1910
MR Type or Builder	MR Type 4c
No. of Levers	33
Ways of Working	AB
Current Status	Active
Listed (Y/N)	Y 2013

Garsdale signal box (Fig. 45) was renamed from Hawes Junction. Until 1959, trains ran to Hawes station, in what is now North Yorkshire, and the line was built by the Midland Railway. From Northallerton the North Eastern Railway (NER) built a branch line from Northallerton to Hawes to form an end-on junction. Part of the line the NER built is now the Wensleydale Railway, cheered on no doubt by Wallace and Gromit. The joint Midland Railway station at Hawes is still there and preserved.

NER engines used to work through to Hawes Junction and they would turn on the turntable there before returning to Northallerton. An engine was turning on the turntable one day in 1900 when

Fig. 43   Blea Moor signal box looking towards Ribblehead viaduct, November 2006.

Fig. 44   Blea Moor signal box looking from Ribblehead viaduct towards Carlisle, November 2006.

Fig. 45   Garsdale (Hawes Junction) signal box, July 2003.

Fig. 46   Garsdale station looking towards Carlisle, July 2003.

a vicious easterly wind caught hold of the loco, causing it to spin round for hours until sand could be poured down the turntable pit to stop it. After that the turntable was surrounded by a stockade of old sleepers.

Hawes Junction has another less amusing claim to fame. In 1910 it was the scene of a tragic railway accident in which twelve people died. The Midland Railway policy of small engines meant that most expresses from Carlisle had to be assisted over Ais Gill summit. The assisting locomotive was detached at Garsdale and there was often more than one loco to go back to Carlisle. On 24 December there were two locos coupled together waiting outside the box for the starter signal to go off so that they could proceed north. The signaller forgot about the two locos and pulled off the signals for a northbound Scottish express. The crew of the two locos thought the signals had been cleared for them and set off. The Scottish express soon caught them up and there was a horrific crash near Mallerstang. As most coaches were gas lit in those days there was a ghastly fire in which some of the passengers were incinerated.

This led to the introduction of lever collars, which are a reminder placed on a lever, and, later, track circuiting. A track circuit is a means of detecting the presence of a vehicle in a track section. This is then used either to show the position on a diagram or interlock block apparatus and signals such that a track cannot be cleared whilst another train is occupying it.

Fig. 46 shows the line curving round to Moorcock viaduct, which then leads to Moorcock tunnel – only 98yds (90m) long – and then Lunds viaduct. The track leading off to the right on the curve is to the up refuge and engineer's sidings. To the right of

Fig. 47   Garsdale station looking towards Settle, July 2003.

that, by the ballast tip, is the trackbed of the Hawes branch.

The station buildings and platforms at Garsdale looking towards Leeds are shown in Fig. 47. The Hawes branch platform is on the far left but is now fenced off by the pseudo Midland Railway palings.

There were a number of cottages built by the Midland Railway at the time of the line's construction. They survive together with others built close to the Moorcock Inn. This community had to rely on church services being held in the station waiting room.

Garsdale station is 256 miles 53 chains (413.1km) from St Pancras.

Fig. 48   Kirkby Stephen signal box, October 2014.

Kirkby Stephen (KS)

Date Built	1974
MR Type or Builder	BR Type LMR 15c
No. of Levers	20
Ways of Working	AB
Current Status	Active
Listed (Y/N)	N

Kirkby Stephen station was originally called Kirkby Stephen West as the NER had already built a station named Kirkby Stephen, which subsequently became Kirkby Stephen East. This line was the Eden Valley Line and closed in 1970. Since 1986, a preservation movement has been reopening the line in stages.

The Network Rail station is well over a mile from the town and perhaps this is partially responsible for fairly low passenger figures of around 30,000 per annum, although there has been an increase in recent years.

The London Midland Region style of flat-roofed architecture in Fig. 48 is not the most appealing on the network but at least it is there.

Fig. 49 is the view towards Carlisle, with the splendid Midland station building on the right. The Friends of the Settle–Carlisle Line (FoSCL) have adopted the station and set up an exhibition in the station building of Midland Railway artefacts. There are two holiday let cottages on the station

Fig. 49   Kirkby Stephen station with the view towards Carlisle, October 2014.

Fig. 50   Kirkby Stephen station with a view past the signal box and goods shed towards Settle, October 2014.

and the refurbished building was declared open by HRH Prince Charles in 2005.

The station is 266 miles 47 chains (429km) from St Pancras.

Looking the other way towards Leeds in the up direction, Fig. 50 shows the surviving goods shed, located just past the signal box. The down refuge siding on the right is all there with its catch points but is literally goods only, as there is only a ground disc to signal exit from the siding. That would not preclude passenger coaches going in there but there couldn't be any passengers aboard.

There are two IBS from Garsdale to Kirkby Stephen in the up direction towards Leeds.

Fig. 51   *Appleby North signal box and junctions, October 2014.*

Appleby North (AN)

Date Built	1951
MR Type or Builder	LMS Type 11c
No. of Levers	25
Ways of Working	AB
Current Status	Active
Listed (Y/N)	N

Appleby is a delightful town and well known in the far northwest for the Appleby Horse Fair – horses have been traded here since 1685 and continue to be so today. Appleby was the historic county town of Westmorland and there is evidence of activity here from the twelfth century. Its main trade now is

tourism with its proximity to the Lake District, Fells and Yorkshire Dales.

Appleby station is still a junction with the former Eden Valley Line, now closed but still surviving as far as Warcop, where a preservation movement has its base.

The signal box appears to be another of the type kept at Crewe during the war years to replace bomb-damaged items but never used then. As with all of Appleby, it appears to be in very good condition. The line to Warcop with a passing loop can be seen going to the right-hand side of the box in Fig. 51, and beyond the box are four sidings. The inner home signal is bracketed out across the running line to counteract the curvature of the line in the

Fig. 53   *Appleby station and heritage centre looking towards Settle, October 2014.*

Fig. 52   *Appleby North signal box towards Carlisle, October 2014.*

Fig. 54   Rear view of Appleby North signal box, November 2006.

Carlisle direction. There are two crossovers in front of the box, a facing and a trailing.

Fig. 52 shows the tall bracket signal on the left for Carlisle and to the right to the Eden Valley Line and Warcop, as well as the sidings. The signal post has a lozenge on it to denote that the track is track circuited. This absolves the driver of a train from calling the signaller to announce the train's presence – rule 55. The period speed restriction sign applies to the branch only. Another class 66 with coal empties is on its way, heading north. Note the single slip in front of the box as we look at it. This enables southbound trains, right-hand track, to reverse into the sidings or to take the Eden Valley Line. The double-decker ground disc signals the points, also when a train is reversing. The lower disc is for the sidings, the upper disc for the crossover.

Fig. 53 could almost be the Midland Railway, with footbridge, station buildings and water tower and water crane on the up, left-hand platform. In the main station building on the right there is a memorial plaque to the Bishop of Wakefield, Eric Treacy, who died at the station some years ago. He was a notable photographer, specializing in the steam age. Just visible is a steam age four-wheel salt wagon on the right, and this is located inside the heritage centre. Behind the heritage centre is

the monolithic Midland Railway goods shed. The man on the platform on the right is hurrying to the opposite platform with hot water and milk for the on-train tea trolley service.

Finally, the back of Appleby North signal box with the toilet block added on and main running lines in front of the box are shown in Fig. 54. Appleby North signal box is 277 miles 34 chains (446.5km) from St Pancras and the station is at an elevation of 525ft (160m).

Kirkby Thore (KT)

Date Built	1994
MR Type or Builder	BR Type Portakabin
No. of Levers	Panel
Ways of Working	AB
Current Status	Active
Listed (Y/N)	N

Kirkby Thore is the base from which gypsum is shipped in bulk. Gypsum is a mineral mined locally and is used in the manufacture of plaster and plasterboard in the construction industry. British

Fig. 55   Kirkby Thore signal box, November 2006.

Gypsum manufactures plaster and plasterboard at Kirkby Thore although their headquarters are in Loughborough, Leicestershire. The company is a subsidiary of the French glass manufacturer Saint-Gobain, who are famous for supplying the glass for the Hall of Mirrors at the Palace of Versailles near Paris.

The layout at Kirkby Thore consists of a trailing crossover, down loop with headshunts and a siding off the loop. The siding is described as being for wagon maintenance and a discharge pad.

The layout is controlled from a panel and there is no mechanically operated equipment here. The box is a pair of Portakabins stacked one on the other, as shown in Fig. 55. Kirkby Thore is 282 miles and 2 chains (453.9km) from St Pancras.

There are no IBS between Kirkby Thore and Appleby or to the next block post signal box, which is Culgaith. Seemingly this is because the sections are relatively short and there would not be enough distance to accommodate two trains within the section and still maintain the separation necessary.

Culgaith (C)

Date Built	1908
MR Type or Builder	MR Type 4a
No. of Levers	16
Ways of Working	AB
Current Status	Active
Listed (Y/N)	N

Culgaith signal box (Fig. 56) is another well-maintained and restored signal box that would appear to have been quietly going about its business over the last 100 years and more.

In March 1930 a local passenger train was making its way from Hellifield to Carlisle and had just passed Culgaith station. After the station is Culgaith tunnel and then shortly after that Waste Bank tunnel, where it met, head-on, a stationary engineer's train that was unloading ballast.

The driver of the local train and one passenger died in the accident and there were eight injuries.

Fig. 56   Culgaith signal box, November 2006.

This could be held up as an example of what can happen when rules are disobeyed. The driver of the passenger train passed the Culgaith starting signal at danger and entered the block section when it was known to be already occupied.

The guard of the engineer's train had laid down detonators behind the train but then taken them up. The detonators provide an unmistakeable mini explosion underneath the wheels of a train and are a universal stop signal.

The train driver, guard or responsible person is also required, under Network Rail rules nowadays, to install a clip some way up the track from the train, across the tracks that simulates the presence of a train. In track circuit block areas this then automatically turn signals to red and thus protects the train.

The signaller was criticized for not positively checking the train before it entered the station although he had placed the home signal to danger.

Back to the recent past now, Fig. 57 shows the view towards Leeds and the trailing crossover. An interesting relic from steam days is the loading gauge post and gallows bracket on the right. These were used to ensure that wagons that had just been loaded would fit under tunnels and bridges. The loading gauge is a measurement of the clearances around a train, with reference to the top of the rails.

The actual gauge is missing; this would have been an arc-shaped piece of metal suspended from the gallows bracket.

Finally at Culgaith, Fig. 58 is looking towards Carlisle and Culgaith tunnel. The signal passed at danger, referred to in the description of the accident above, is the semaphore home signal just before the tunnel. The remains of the up station platform can be seen with a converted station building on it. The grand Midland Railway style of 'Derby Gothic' that we have seen so much of is not repeated here, as Culgaith station was built four years after the line was completed. Originally Culgaith had no station but the local clergy objected and so one was built. It closed in 1970 but there are rumblings for its reopening.

Culgaith signal box is 284 miles and 55 chains (458.2km) from St Pancras.

Fig. 57   Culgaith looking towards Leeds, November 2006.

Low House Crossing (LH)

Date Built	1900
MR Type or Builder	MR Type 2b
No. of Levers	12
Ways of Working	AB
Current Status	Active
Listed (Y/N)	N

Low House Crossing (Fig. 59), together with other signal boxes, features on Visit Cumbria's web site, which is helpful if a visit is planned. The box lies on a sharp curve in the track and a deeply wooded area.

Even as picturesque and tranquil a scene as this signal box occupies a place in history for yet another railway accident, of which the Settle–Carlisle Line has had more than its fair share.

At Little Salkeld cutting, which is a few miles from Low House, on 19 January 1918 the 08.50 St Pancras to Glasgow express ran into a landslip that was blocking both tracks. The train was travelling at about 60mph (100km/h) and the resulting crash telescoped the front two coaches, killing seven people and injuring forty-six.

Fig. 58   Culgaith looking towards Carlisle, November 2006.

Fig. 59   Low House Crossing signal box, October 2014.

Fig. 60   Rear of Low House Crossing signal box, November 2006.

Fig. 61   Low House Crossing looking towards Leeds, November 2006.

Fig. 62   Low House Crossing looking towards Carlisle, October 2014.

There had been very severe frosts that winter and a sudden thaw caused the cutting to give way and collapse onto the track. A track worker who had walked past the site minutes before the accident reported that all appeared to be in order.

It was the practice of many companies to plant shrubs and trees on cuttings to stabilize the earthworks and hold it together. In recent times 'leaves on the line' have meant that much of this undergrowth has been cut back in an effort to reduce he amount of vegetation on the track. As long as the root system is not disturbed all should be well.

The rear of Low House Crossing signal box is shown in Fig. 60. There is a small window to the rear to keep an eye on the traffic as the road sweeps round from behind the trees. The corrugated hut would be a lamp hut, a relic of the times when signallers were obliged to fill oil lamps for signals on a regular basis. The later type would go for a week between fillings. The lamps are either converted oil lamps with bulbs in or LED types, which in addition to being more reliable, use less power.

Looking back towards Armathwaite station and Leeds, the superelevation or cant of the track is quite clear (Fig. 61). It is this property of centripetal force, where an object will cling to a curved surface, that was exemplified by the 'Wall of Death' motorbike sideshow principle used in the Virgin Pendolino trains. These trains artificially introduce superelevation to enable them to go round curves faster. The British APT train was a forerunner with this technology but was cancelled as a cost-cutting move. Britain subsequently bought trains using the same principle from the Italians.

Fig. 62 shows Low House Crossing and the home signal with a sighting board. Signal arms have generally been lowered over the years on health and safety grounds where such lowering would not compromise the train driver's view of the signal.

Low House Crossing signal box is 299 miles and 55 chains (482.3km) from St Pancras station.

Howe and Co.'s Siding (HS)

Date Built	1916
MR Type or Builder	Midland Type 4a
No. of Levers	30
Way of Working	AB
Current Status	Active
Listed (Y/N)	N

This area, a few miles from Carlisle, was noteworthy for brick and tile works and plaster manufacturing, all of which are no longer with us here. The nearest station, at Cumwhinton, closed in 1970 although there is agitation now for it to be reopened.

'Howe and Co.' were in the business of gypsum quarrying. The works were closed when they became part of British Gypsum and the main site for gypsum concentrated on Kirkby Thore (*see* Kirkby Thore section).

The signal box is now just a block post with a goods loop and a pair of crossovers to enable both tracks to access the loop.

The box, shown in Fig. 63, is another example of sensitive restoration that still has a vital task to perform and provide a modern working environment for the occupant.

The home signal in Fig. 64 appears to have been lowered on the post. The double-decker ground signals are reasonably common – the lower signal is for nearer movement and the upper signal the movement further away. The goods loop is described as both up and down as there are crossovers to enable access to the loop from either running line.

Howe and Co.'s signal box is 302 miles and 77 chains (487.6km) from St Pancras.

After the signal box the line continues past the closed Cumwhinton station and the line joins the former North Eastern Railway, latterly LNER, at Petteril Bridge junction, 307 miles 12 chains (494.3km) from St Pancras. With seven railway companies running into Carlisle it is not surprising that railways shared tracks at some point. The Midland Railway had its own locomotive depot at Durranhill but shared Carlisle Citadel station with the other companies.

Manchester to Sheffield

Mention those two places together and perhaps thoughts turn to the LNER Woodhead electrified route that closed in 1981. It was used almost exclusively to transport coal from the south Yorkshire coalfield to Manchester and beyond.

The Midland Railway line has survived. The railway scene around Manchester is very complicated, and we shall begin the journey at the

Fig. 63 (left)   Howe and Co.'s Siding signal box, October 2014.

Fig. 64 (below)   Howe and Co.'s siding and crossover, November 2006.

first Midland Railway box, Romiley Junction. The boxes before that are of Lancashire and Yorkshire and Great Central Railway origins. The destination stations for the line are Manchester Piccadilly and Sheffield Midland, now just called Sheffield.

From the suburbs of Manchester to the Peak District in Derbyshire the line ran almost in parallel with the LNWR part of the way as both companies strived to establish a presence in Buxton with its two identical stations side by side. The Duke of Devonshire had insisted that the stations be in keeping with each other and with the town. Only the LNWR station and signal box survives, although the Midland Railway connects by a freight only line.

The scenery in the Peak District is Pennine splendour without the wildness and untamed nature of the Settle–Carlisle. The line is very popular with walkers and hikers as it connects many outdoor pursuit hotspots and yet is near large centres of population.

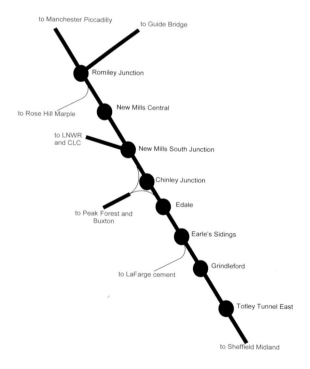

Fig. 65   Manchester to Sheffield, Midland Railway.

Paradoxically the peaceful scenery of the line is not only beautiful but busy with freight traffic in a way not usually encountered in the twenty-first century.

The line continues past the Buxton junction at Chinley to the foothills of the Pennines and a long tunnel before emerging into Yorkshire and a more upmarket suburb of Sheffield before running into Sheffield Midland station.

The modern scene is a variable one, with track circuit block in evidence in some parts as well as absolute block and semaphores.

Romiley Junction (RJ)

Date Built	1899
MR Type or Builder	Midland Type 2b
No. of Levers	OCS panel
Way of Working	TCB
Current Status	Active
Listed (Y/N)	N

Romiley Junction signal box (Fig. 66) may date from the century before last but its defences are bang up to date. Many signal boxes have been attacked and some even burned down during the rise of anti-social behaviour in the 1990s and beyond. In an urban context these precautions are all too necessary, but in more rural locations it was quite usual for the signal box key to be placed on a hook on the signal box steps. This meant that a relief signaller could easily gain access to the box.

OCS stands for one control switch, and this enables a route to be set up complete with signals by pressing one switch. Such panels are not suitable for complicated track layouts. There are also individual switches to set up a route not normally used.

The signaller can still use the walkway around the box for cultivation, however. The Romiley Junction maroon enamelled sign above the door is a steam age relic – quite a few boxes in this area sport these items.

The Romiley Junction in the signal box name is ahead in Fig. 67. This is a double junction rather than the single-lead junction we saw at Settle. It is

Fig. 66   Romiley Junction signal box, August 2006.

Fig. 67   Romiley Junction with Ashburys and Denton tracks ahead, August 2006.

clearly much busier here. Left goes to Ashburys Junction, while straight on goes to Guide Bridge. There is a small branch line south of Romiley Junction that goes to Rose Hill, Marple. From Marple trains take the Guide Bridge branch.

Ashburys Junction is the dividing point for Manchester Piccadilly (LNWR) or Manchester Victoria (L&Y) stations.

The Guide Bridge route can end up at Ashburys but there is another option for Stalybridge, which then leads across the Pennines to Yorkshire.

The multiple aspect signal RJ21 has no track circuit lozenge on it, presumably as nearly all MAS signals operate by track circuits. The period stencil 20mph restriction sign refers to the Ashburys branch.

Fig. 68 shows Romiley main station building but is only about half of it as the station is four storeys high at street level. There is some contention that the station building is of Great Central Railway origin but, as the Midland ran here and there were connections to the L&YR and the LNWR, perhaps it could safely be called a joint station.

Fig. 68   Romiley station building, August 2006.

New Mills Central (NM)

Date Built	1924
MR Type or Builder	Midland Type 4d+
No. of Levers	30
Way of Working	TCB
Current Status	Active
Listed (Y/N)	N

New Mills Central signal box is shown in Fig. 69 and is in a remarkably hemmed-in location. The box is showing its age although it is another of these boxes designed by the Midland Railway but not brought into service until after the LMS was a reality. The stove appears to be modern replacement and the roof slates are suffering. The brick building to the right of the box is probably a relay room as track circuit block needs such rooms to store all the track circuit relays that control the colour light signals. The box has a thirty-lever frame but all the controls are electrical. This means that the levers just operate switches to control points and signals. The interlocking in this case is always electrical or electronic.

The road overbridge and railway footbridge almost collide at New Mills Central station in Fig. 70. The signal box can just be seen beyond the road overbridge. The line is shown heading off towards Sheffield. The tunnel mouth to the left is from the closed Hayfield Branch, which was a Great Central Railway possession.

New Mills Central station is shown in Fig. 71, which looks back towards Manchester. The layout here is simple, with a trailing crossover and refuge siding on the up side towards Sheffield.

The LNWR is sufficiently close in its parallel line to Buxton to have a station at New Mills Newtown.

New Mills Central is 173 miles 11 chains (278.6km) from St Pancras via Leicester, Chaddesdon and Millers Dale. The fact that this direct route of the Midland Railway from London to Manchester closed in 1967 does not affect the modern view of distances.

New Mills South Junction (NS)

Date Built	1903
MR Type or Builder	Midland Type 3b+
No. of Levers	55
Way of Working	AB
Current Status	Active
Listed (Y/N)	N

New Mills South Junction signal box is depicted in Fig. 72 and appears to be in splendid isolation at the start of the Peak District scenic area. As well as the scenery, the railway operating environment changes and we are back in absolute block territory.

Fig. 69   New Mills Central signal box, July 2005.

Fig. 70   New Mills station looking towards Sheffield, July 2005.

Fig. 71   New Mills Central station looking towards Manchester, July 2005.

Fig. 72   New Mills South Junction signal box, July 2005.

The junction is formed by a line that is made up of two routes as shown on the schematic diagram, Fig. 65. The other line of the junction is the original line we have been following from Romiley. The route then continues for a while until the next junction at Chinley.

Although New Mills South Junction signal box has been heavily modernized it still shouts Midland Railway. The typical Midland frame is in view, with some levers painted white out of use. To the right of the walkway on the opposite side of the tracks to the box is the relay room, used to accommodate the track circuit relays, which are physically large and enclosed in glass cases. They are known by signallers and technicians as 'fish tanks'. Relays are present in everyday life and perhaps the most common application is the modern car, where many different services are switched by relays. A relay enables circuits to be controlled by electric power at a distance and the power to control is

usually a fraction of the power to be switched. Relays have few working parts and are therefore usually very reliable.

The junction, then, is a double one that incorporates a goods loop.

Fig. 73 is the view of the tracks from Stockport and Northenden on the right, curving round towards Chinley Junction and Sheffield. The line on the left is the up main line from Romiley and is termed the up goods loop according to TrackMaps, but is clearly used to hold passenger trains as it has a normal-sized starter signal. There is a facing crossover further up the line so that a train can be held in the loop but another train can pass in the same direction. The down Romiley connection is much further up the line past the box. There is another facing crossover to enable trains heading for Romiley to cross over from the Chinley direction, which is signalled by the branch or 'feather' on the colour light signal.

Fig. 73   New Mills South Junction looking towards Sheffield, July 2005.

Fig. 74   New Mills South Junction looking towards Manchester, July 2005.

Fig. 74 shows the crossover referred to above that connects the up line from Romiley to Chinley Junction to leave the goods loop to continue on the left as in Fig. 73. The bracket signal left-hand arm, as viewed, is for the crossover to the up line to Sheffield and the right-hand arm is for the up goods loop.

New Mills South Junction signal box is 172 miles 17 chains (277.1km) from St Pancras.

Chinley Junction (CY)

Date Built	1980
MR Type or Builder	BR, LMR Type 15c
No. of Levers	OCS panel
Way of Working	TCB, AB
Current Status	Active
Listed (Y/N)	N

Chinley station was of some importance while it was the junction of two double-track main lines: the lines from Manchester to London and from Manchester to Sheffield met here. This meant that Chinley station was a large and busy station with six platforms in all. In 1967 the Midland Main Line to London was truncated after Peak Forest and closed to passengers. This demoted Chinley station to be an island platform on the purely Manchester to Sheffield line.

The one control switch in the signal box panel has switches that would set a route up by correctly changing all points and signals in its path. In addition the panel is equipped with individual switches for each function that can be used if the route set up on the single switch did not obey for some reason, or if there was a move needed for which there was no discrete switch.

The panel also contains the absolute block instruments for communication with New Mills South Junction, Edale towards Sheffield and Peak Forest South towards the erstwhile London connection, shown in Fig. 73.

There was an accident here in 1986, involving an inexperienced signaller caught up in an extraordinary set of circumstances.

Before the incident there had been a total electrical power failure. While the point motors are hydraulically operated, they are electrically controlled, which meant that the signaller had to go out to the point motors and manually crank the hydraulic motor to the required position. Unfortunately, although a train's progress through the track circuits is tracked by red lights moving across the panel, the actual route set was not shown. After power was restored a track circuit refused to reset to normal and locked the position of points. The result of these failures eventually caused a collision between a pair of diesel locomotives coupled together and a passenger train. Unfortunately the driver of the passenger train was killed. The

Fig. 75   Chinley Junction signal box, October 2014.

Fig. 76   Chinley Junction signal box close up, August 2006.

Fig. 77   Chinley Junction signal box surrounded by infrastructure, October 2014.

electrical fault with the track circuit relay was traced to a fuse contact.

Fig. 75 shows Chinley Junction signal box perched at the point at which the line from Manchester diverges to Peak Forest South. The facing crossover enables trains travelling in the Sheffield direction to access the Peak Forest line. There is a similar arrangement 7 chains (140m) from the box for the line in the Manchester direction. Both lines to Peak Forest meet at a point and the line then bifurcates to double track to Peak Forest.

Fig. 76 is the box face with a venerable-looking wooden name plate with modern unrelieved brickwork. The extension down the other end of the building is the relay room, necessary in TCB areas. The woodwork could do with a makeover and the sunshield part of the roof is in poor condition.

Finally at Chinley, Fig. 77 shows the side view, and it becomes apparent why the box appears hemmed in by the ancillary buildings with the fence at the side.

Despite the loss of passenger services after the London route closed there is considerable freight traffic past the box, with services from Peak Forest and Earle's Sidings further on towards Sheffield. Chinley Junction signal box is 168 miles 39 chains (271.2km) from St Pancras.

Edale (EE)

Date Built	1893
MR Type or Builder	Midland Type 2b+
No. of Levers	20
Way of Working	AB
Current Status	Active
Listed (Y/N)	N

Edale signal box (Fig. 78) occupies a scenic spot in the Peak District that is popular with walkers and tourists. The station gives details of the many local beauty spots and the station café is run by the National Trust. Edale is widely recognized as the southerly starting point for the Pennine Way walk. The village has two pubs and lies in a picturesque setting.

The box at Edale is accompanied by the inevitable relay room and is unusual in that the staircase enters the box from the rear. The box is in good, modernized condition. It used to control a refuge siding on the up side towards Sheffield and a goods loop on the down side. The layout did not permit these facilities to be of any appreciable length and would not appear to be long enough to contain modern-length freight trains, so consequently the facilities have fallen into disuse.

Fig. 78   Edale signal box, October 2014.

Fig. 79 depicts the line curving away from the station platforms in the Sheffield direction. The yellow gadget by the signal arm on the right is a position indicator transmitter that shows the position of the signal to the signaller in the box.

Indeed, the down line on the left curvature is so tight that it requires double check rails. Check rails are there to contain a vehicle that is derailed at speed on a curve to save it from a worse fate, and they also help to reduce flange and rail wear. The bridge structure that the rails cross over just at the platform ends is an underpass to connect the platforms, as there is no footbridge here. It is typical Midland Railway in its luxurious use of hewn stone, as is the platform face.

Fig. 80 looks the other way towards Manchester, with Edale signal box on the right. The up refuge siding and buffer stop, on the right, are still there but there is no longer any connection to the running line. The down side loop is still connected at the Manchester end only. A train is expected on the down line (it was a class 66 with stone train). The tunnel in the distance is the Cowburn tunnel, 2 miles and 182 yards (3.4km) in length. Edale signal box is 169 miles 34 chains (272.7km) from St Pancras and the station is a quarter-mile or 20 chains (400m) east of the box.

As an epilogue at Edale, Fig. 81 shows the bracket signal canted out over the track to give the train driver an earlier view after rounding the curve into the platform. Just behind the bracket signal is a black-faced, yellow-striped ground signal, which is used to allow a train to pass a signal that may be on (at danger). This is to allow shunting moves to take place without the signaller having to repetitively change the signal aspect. They are normally only found where the signaller has the piece of track in plain sight, as in this case.

Fig. 79   Edale signal box looking towards Sheffield, October 2014.

Fig. 80   Edale signal box looking towards Manchester, October 2014.

Fig. 81   Edale and a train from Manchester, October 2014.

Fig. 82   Earle's Sidings signal box, October 2014.

Earle's Sidings (ES)

Date Built	1929
MR Type or Builder	Midland Type 4e+
No. of Levers	35
Way of Working	AB
Current Status	Active
Listed (Y/N)	N

There is no station here but there is an extensive cement works owned by the Lafarge company. Lafarge is a multinational company of French origin who first took off as world players in cement when they won the contract for the Suez Canal in the nineteenth century.

Limestone is an important constituent of the cement process and the Peak District has it in abundance.

There are seven sidings, a goods loop and a run-round loop so the place has the appearance of a busy goods yard.

Fig. 82 depicts a box that is recognizably Midland Railway but with a flat roof in the style of 1950s London Midland Region. There was a fire at the box in 1976 and the box acquired its flat roof then. The down home signal by the box has a sighting board. The running lines run right in front of the box and the previously described layout is across the tracks from those.

Fig. 83 is the view from an overbridge at the far end of the layout looking towards Manchester. The class 158 is on its way to Sheffield on the up line. The up starter goods signal for trains out of the reception loop can clearly be seen, as can the double slip point arrangement in front of the signal. A double slip is the equivalent of a scissors cross-over, which is like two crossovers laid on top of one another with a diamond crossing in the middle. It permits any line to cross over. They are fairly rare now except in large passenger stations and there

Fig. 83   Earle's Sidings and a train to Sheffield, October 2014.

Fig. 84   Earle's Sidings cement works starter signal, August 2006.

Grindleford (GD)

Date Built	1938
MR Type or Builder	LMS Type 11c
No. of Levers	25
Way of Working	AB
Current Status	Active
Listed (Y/N)	N

are two here – the second one is at the other end of the layout. They are used to save space and are only of use where the speeds are low.

At the other end of the layout the line to the Lafarge cement works curves away to the left and has a single check rail on it (Fig. 84). The starter signal guards the exit from the line.

In Fig. 85 the class 185 hurries towards Manchester past Earle's Sidings with a First Transpennine Express service.

The other double slip on the layout, which was scheduled for change out at the second survey visit, is shown in Fig. 86. The Lafarge branch with check rail is seen on the right. This view is facing towards Manchester.

Grindleford is the last stop in Derbyshire. The cavernous Totley tunnel just by the station announces that it was built in 1883; it is 3 miles and 950 yards long (5.7km), and at the other end is Yorkshire.

The Grindleford station building survives as a café and this establishment is particularly popular with walkers and hikers, serving traditional fare at economical prices.

The station appears to be a two-platform halt type but that is because the station building is away up at road level above the railway.

Grindleford signal box is an LMS creation that has been modernized but with an extraordinarily complicated set of box steps. It was refurbished in 2005 and so the 2006 picture (Fig. 87) shows the box looking in good condition. The view is towards Manchester and there is a small fan of sidings by the box that appear disused.

Grindleford station is shown in Fig. 88 looking towards Manchester from the Totley tunnel portal; the station building is off to the left up the bank.

Fig. 85   Earle's Sidings and First TransPennine class 185, 185 107 train bound for Manchester, August 2006.

Fig. 86   Earle's Sidings and a double slip crossing, October 2014.

Fig. 87 *Grindleford signal box, June 2006.*

Fig. 88 *Grindleford station, June 2006.*

Fig. 89 is a close-up view of a home signal on the up side at Grindleford, guarding the route to Sheffield. The signal is electrically operated and although the rear faces away from the signal box, there is a backlight cover. There is no position indicator transmitter as that is integral with the electrical motor equipment.

Fig. 90 is the Grindleford station building with London Midland Region steam era enamel sign. The café does a roaring trade with walkers and tourists.

Totley Tunnel East (TE)

Date Built	1893
MR Type or Builder	Midland Type 2b
No. of Levers	12
Way of Working	AB, TCB
Current Status	Active
Listed (Y/N)	N

The other end of Totley tunnel leads us to the first and last signal box in Yorkshire on this line, shown

Fig. 89 (left) *Grindleford and the Sheffield-bound starter, June 2006.*

Fig. 90 (below) *Grindleford station building, June 2006.*

Fig. 91 Totley Tunnel East signal box, Sheffield, June 2006.

in Fig. 91. The line splits after the box, with one track going to Sheffield Midland station and the other south towards Chesterfield.

The box works absolute block to Grindleford and track circuit block to Sheffield power box. The box is 154 miles 62 chains (249.1km) from St Pancras.

Peterborough to Syston

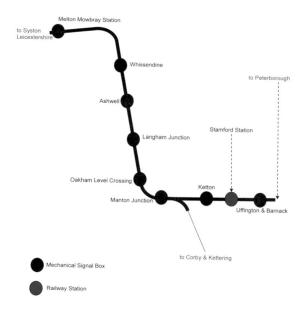

Fig. 92 Peterborough–Syston line.

The Midland Railway spread its tentacles far and wide, reaching the fringes of East Anglia at Peterborough.

The Midland was to penetrate even as far east as Norfolk later in a collaborative company with the Great Northern Railway – the Midland and Great Northern Joint Railway. A fragment of this railway survives as the preserved North Norfolk Railway.

The journey begins nearer the Peterborough end at Uffington and ends at Melton Mowbray station. From there to Syston junction and Leicester there is no mechanical signalling.

The land is pleasantly undulating and typical mid-shires England scenery.

Uffington and Barnack (UN)

Date Built	1909
MR Type or Builder	Midland Type 4A
No. of Levers	16
Way of Working	AB, TCB
Current Status	Active
Listed (Y/N)	N

Uffington and Barnack in Cambridgeshire had its own railway station, though the station closed to passenger traffic in 1952 and freight in 1964.

The box in Fig. 93 is substantially original in looks except for the lack of roof finials on the ridge tiles. The fire bucket hooks near the steps are an original feature. The steps are galvanized steel and perhaps a better view is of the period 'Beware of Trains' cast iron sign. Once commonplace, these are now quite rare in the wild although there are many in captivity in private hands as collector's items. The box has lost its full name plate.

Uffington and Barnack stationmaster's house is in the background in Fig. 94, together with the manual wooden crossing gates. The gates overlap as the road aperture is larger than the railway one.

The Uffington and Barnack signaller is off to close the gates in Fig. 95. There is a trailing cross-over here and part of the point rodding can just be seen.

Fig. 93 *Uffington and Barnack signal box, July 2006.*

Fig. 94 *Uffington and Barnack former station building, July 2006.*

Stamford Station

Just in Lincolnshire, Stamford station (Fig. 96) does have a signal box but it is a retired one, so that will be retained for another day. The main interest is the station building – a rare delight. The station is in the mock Tudor style after the real Tudor style at Burghley House nearby.

Ketton (K)

Date Built	1900
MR Type or Builder	Midland Type 2b
No. of Levers	20
Way of Working	AB
Current Status	Active
Listed (Y/N)	N

Ketton, the next signal box, is the first excursion into Rutland, England's smallest county.

One mile (1.6km) up the line from the signal box is Ketton cement works, which was established in 1928, became Castle Cement and is now owned by the Hanson Group. There is a fan of four loops leading to loading silos and another run-round loop. Entry to the Ketton cement complex is by local ground frame although the ground frame is usually released by the local signal box, so movements remain supervised.

Fig. 95 *Uffington and Barnack signal box and signaller, July 2006.*

Fig. 96 *Stamford station, Lincolnshire, July 2006.*

Fig. 97   Ketton signal box, July 2006.

In Fig. 97 the Ketton signal box looks almost original except for the steps. Cultivation is well under way. There is a trailing crossover just the other side of the crossing, and instead of a ground disc there is an LED indicator signal at the foot of the box. The yellow three-quarter-mile post announces that the box is 6 miles 60 chains (10.9km) from Manton Junction.

Fig. 98 shows Ketton signal box looking towards Manton Junction; in the distance is a colour light signal and a semaphore.

Manton Junction (MJ)

Date Built	1913
MR Type or Builder	Midland Type 4c+
No. of Levers	Nx Panels
Way of Working	AB, TCB
Current Status	Active
Listed (Y/N)	N

Manton Junction is in the county of Rutland and nowadays it is in rural isolation, although there was a station and goods yard here with a small community to support the railway. The villages of Manton and Wing are some way off.

The station closed in 1966 and the remaining buildings were given over to light industrial use. Passenger services down the Corby and Kettering line were withdrawn and only reinstated in 2009. There is now talk of redoubling the Corby and Kettering line. Corby (in Northamptonshire) had a large steel manufacturing works. Steel making finished in 1981 with many job losses, but a tube works remains, supplied with steel from Teesside and South Wales. Manton Junction controls the freight line to Corby.

In Fig. 99 the 749yd (685m) Manton tunnel is in the background. The line to Melton Mowbray and Syston runs into the tunnel. but before it does that it is joined by the Corby and Kettering line that runs behind the box.

Fig. 100 goes inside the box at Manton Junction. The signaller's operating position consists of two Nx, or eNtrance eXit, panels. As the name suggests they consist of an entry and exit whose passage by

Fig. 98   Ketton signal box looking towards Manton Junction, July 2006.

Fig. 99   Manton Junction signal box, July 2006.

Fig. 100   Manton Junction signal box Nx panels, July 2006.

a train is set up by a single switch for a given route. The panel is made up of a matrix of aluminium sockets into which can be inserted plastic tiles until a track diagram is built up. Some of the tiles contain switches and/or lights or text so the diagram is interactive.

While every set of tiles that make up a diagram will have bespoke elements to it to reflect the location, it is fairly easy to make changes. Such panels are manufactured by TEW at Nottingham.

There are two Nx panels at Manton Junction, the nearer for the actual junction and the one further away for the Corby steel tube manufacturing plant.

Fig. 101 shows the side and rear of Manton Junction, with the Kettering and Corby line on the left. There is genuine light at the end of the tunnel and it is not an oncoming train.

Looking the other way now, Fig. 102 shows the Kettering and Corby line on the right splitting into two after the single-lead junction. The line to Peterborough curves away to the left with the remnants of the passenger and freight facilities in the triangle in front of the box. The signaller's trusty Baby Belling cooker is on the right.

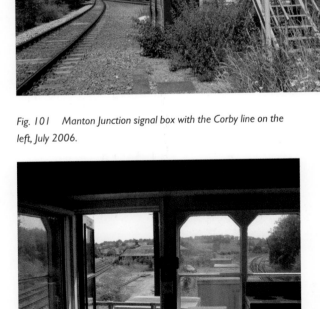

Fig. 101   Manton Junction signal box with the Corby line on the left, July 2006.

Fig. 102   Manton Junction signal box looking across the former goods yard and station areas, July 2006.

Fig. 103 Oakham Level Crossing signal box, July 2006.

Fig. 104 Oakham station, July 2006.

Oakham Level Crossing (OA)

Date Built	1899
MR Type or Builder	Midland Type 2b
No. of Levers	17
Way of Working	AB
Current Status	Active
Listed (Y/N)	Y

Our third stop in the county of Rutland is a signal box famous for over sixty years as the prototype for the Airfix OO gauge model railway signal box kit, still in production by Dapol. The original price was 2/- or 10p but there has been a price rise over the years. The box is now a listed building (but the proper place for the fire buckets is by the steps). It has been very sympathetically restored and looks authentic.

Fig. 104 shows a fine cast iron frame for the awning and behind that is an equally fine station building. The view is towards Melton Mowbray, and the start of the up goods loops can be seen just after the platform. Just up the line on the goods loop is the Cemetery Siding. The siding has a scotch-block fitted, which is a device across at least one rail that prevents a vehicle from entering or leaving the siding – rather like a buffer stop in the middle of a piece of track but moveable.

Fig. 105 Rear view of Oakham signal box, July 2006.

Fig. 106 Oakham station, view of staggered platforms, July 2006.

Looking at the rear of the box in Fig. 105, there is some extra detail for those who wish to bring their Airfix model up to date.

Looking back, there are staggered platform arrangements at Oakham station (Fig. 106). The footbridge is another fine Midland Railway product. Oakham station is 93 miles 61 chains (150.9km) from St Pancras via Corby.

Langham Junction (LJ)

Date Built	1890
MR Type or Builder	Midland Type 2a
No. of Levers	20
Way of Working	AB
Current Status	Active
Listed (Y/N)	N

Fig. 107   Langham Junction signal box, July 2006.

Langham Junction was never a junction at all but the Midland Railway termed it thus when they upgraded the tracks between Oakham and Langham to quadruple track in 1891; nowadays the extra tracks are described as goods loops. They are, however, about a mile long and of some use as such, as freight trains can be of prodigious length.

The area was rich in ironstone and in those days it all went by rail. This ironstone field stretched from north Oxfordshire near Banbury to Northamptonshire, Lincolnshire and High Dyke on the East Coast Main Line. It was the reason the Corby steelworks was established in the 1960s. Unfortunately the ironstone was mostly economically exhausted by the late 1960s and completely defunct by 1979. In common with most areas of Britain, there was also a coalfield in Rutland, further adding to minerals traffic.

Fig. 107 shows a box that has survived, although curiously the windows at the ends do not go to the full length at the first floor level as the front windows do. The staircase is at the rear, which is unusual. The bird feeders are another signaller pastime in evidence here.

Fig. 108 shows the signal box with the bracket signal home and Oakham's distant signal. The smaller arm permits entry into the up goods loop.

Fig. 108   Langham Junction signal box bracket signal, July 2006.

Fig. 109   Langham Junction signal box extended goods loops, July 2007.

This bracket signal was replaced in 2009 with another semaphore installation. Note how the guy wires are trying to maintain equilibrium.

Looking back towards Oakham and the goods loop in Fig. 109, note that there is a set of catch points on the up, left-hand side. These are spring-loaded and will derail any vehicle that is running away back towards the camera and the running lines. In theory, these are not required any longer as all vehicles are supposed to automatically apply the brakes if they are uncoupled or if the air brake pipes are disconnected. However, there are such things as the gangers' trolleys, which are not so equipped. At the other end of the loop will be trap

points that perform a similar function but are operated in tandem with the siding exit point lever in the signal box. You can probably just make out the trap points on the down, right-hand side but most of it is obstructed by the ballast pile.

Looking at Langham Junction signal box from the rear in Fig. 110, that unusual staircase position is clearly evident. The bird theme is continued round the back with bird box and what looks like house martin or swift nests under the eaves.

Langham Junction signal box is 95 miles 6 chains (153km) from St Pancras via Corby.

Ashwell

Date Built	1912
MR Type or Builder	Midland Type 4a
No. of Levers	25
Way of Working	AB
Current Status	Active
Listed (Y/N)	N

Ashwell was an early recipient of traffic as a result of the reactivation of ironstone quarrying after the line was built. The major deposits were found a couple of miles from Ashwell station and were so near the surface that they could be scooped up and carted to Ashwell goods yard for onward shipment. After a

Fig. 110   Rear of Langham Junction signal box, July 2007.

while a branch line was built in 1882 and a complex of lines, both standard and narrow gauge, sprang up to service the quarries named Cottesmore, South, Exton Park and Burley. The remains of these workings form the Rutland Railway Museum.

Ashwell signal box is another along the line that controls a crossing as well as being a block post. The box (Fig. 111) appears well looked after and sympathetically modernized except for the galvanized steel steps, which are side mounted in this case.

Ashwell signal box and the line back towards Oakham are shown in Fig. 112 – a mixture of colour light and semaphore home signals.

Fig. 113 looks towards Melton Mowbray and Syston. The remains of the up station platform are in evidence – the station closed to passengers in 1966.

The goods shed can just be seen behind the tree and it appears to be at right angles to the running line; this is in fact the case, and very unusually wagons would be turned on a wagon turntable to make the 90-degree turn to get into the shed. This arrangement was commonplace in restricted areas such as dock line and narrow gauge railways, where space was always tight. The branch to the ironstone quarries came in before the home signal and on that side of the line. The home signal has its counter-balance weight halfway up the post just by the track circuit lozenge.

Ashwell signal box is 99 miles 69 chains (160.7km) from St Pancras via Corby.

Fig. 111   Ashwell signal box bracket signal, July 2007.

Fig. 112   Ashwell signal box looking towards Oakham, July 2007.

Fig. 113   Ashwell signal box looking towards Syston, July 2007.

Fig. 114   Whissendine signal box, July 2007.

Fig. 115   Rear of Whissendine signal box, July 2007.

Whissendine

Date Built	1940
MR Type or Builder	Midland Type 4d
No. of Levers	20
Way of Working	AB
Current Status	Active
Listed (Y/N)	N

Whissendine had a station but this lasted less time than most, as the station and box were over a mile from the village. In addition, cottages built for railway workers were nearer to Ashwell station than their own. Whissendine station closed to both passengers and goods in March 1955.

Whissendine signal box (Fig. 114) is of World War II ancestry and consequently has a brick-built frame room on the ground floor, all the better to withstand bomb blast damage. There are no frame room windows thus minimizing the risk of injury to occupants from flying glass in an attack.

Whissendine signal box is seen from the rear in Fig. 115, and there's plenty of evidence of a bird lover within, with feeders and box. Even though this box was built seventeen years after the Midland Railway ceased to exist, the influences are there.

Melton Mowbray Station (MM)

Date Built	1942
MR Type or Builder	LMS Type 11C
No. of Levers	45
Way of Working	AB, TCB
Current Status	Active
Listed (Y/N)	N

Melton Mowbray in Leicestershire is an ancient borough that is close to the Fosse Way, a Roman road and backbone of communications in the Midlands. It has many listed buildings and has a market that was first mentioned in the Domesday Book. Nowadays it is most renowned as a foodie centre, famous for its pork pies, and a centre of Stilton cheese production. Stilton is actually a village in Huntingdonshire but the cheese was so named as that was the cheese's destination after manufacture.

The Melton Mowbray pork pie has gained European recognition in much the same way as Parma ham or champagne.

Melton Mowbray station is most renowned for the luxury of its conveniences and the fact that hot-water pipes were provided to heat the first class waiting room toilet white goods.

Fig. 116   Melton Mowbray Station signal box, July 2007.

Fig. 117   Rear of Melton Mowbray Station signal box, July 2007.

point at the head of the sidings. These are often used in low-speed areas to save space. There are no windows in the rear to keep an eye on shunting moves, though.

Fig. 118 shows the view towards Syston and Leicester. Note the bracket home signal low down on the post. The track coming towards the camera leads to a disused end loading bay, where a vehicle could be driven onto a railway wagon. Further up the line on the right-hand side there is a branch to Asfordby as was, which is now Alstom's Midlands Test Centre.

Melton Mowbray station is a study in minor Midland magnificence (Fig. 119). Given the station's relatively minor status, the message is that progress has resulted in a station of substance from a company of stature.

In its current context the signal box (Fig. 116) seems a bit odd, but there used to be a fan of sidings just behind it and consequently a need for an overhanging design. The LNWR and GWR also had these structures where the box footprint was narrow.

The signal box is shown from the rear in Fig. 117, and you can see some of the sidings were still in place in 2006. Note there is a tandem or three-way

Fig. 118   Melton Mowbray station looking towards Syston and Leicester, July 2007.

Fig. 119   Melton Mowbray station, July 2007.

Fig. 120   Melton Mowbray looking towards Peterborough and the goods loops, July 2007.

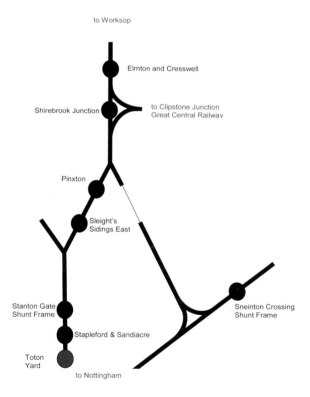

Fig. 121   Worksop–Nottingham schematic diagram.

Looking back towards Peterborough (Fig. 120), note the down goods loop has a sighting board starter, as has the running line.

Worksop to Nottingham

The Midland Railway's *raison d'être* was carrying coal, and this line was right in the thick of it. The coalfields around Worksop were always extremely productive and the yards at Toton near Nottingham one of the country's largest for marshalling coal trains for onward transmission to London and elsewhere. The yards at Toton still exist but now take on other duties. These are centres for ballast stocks as virtual quarries, wagon storage and track-laying and maintenance-vehicle stabling, and the DB Schenker depot.

Starting from the first Midland Railway box at Elmton and Creswell in Derbyshire, we end up at Toton Yard in Nottinghamshire, including one Midland box, at Sneinton, which strictly speaking is off our route but physically close to it.

Fig. 122   Elmton and Creswell Junction signal box, June 2008.

Elmton and Creswell (EC)

Date Built	1942
MR Type or Builder	LMS Type 11C
No. of Levers	48
Way of Working	AB Switched Out
Current Status	Closed
Listed (Y/N)	N

Creswell was always associated with coal mining and was the scene of one of the worst post-war mining disasters when an underground fire cost eighty miners their lives. There has always been another cost to coal mining.

The original station closed in 1964 but has subsequently reopened as just Creswell. There was a junction here with a line to Staveley near Chesterfield and this was associated with the movement of coal from Oxcroft and Bolsover collieries. There was also the Seymour stocking site for coal, which was a mini marshalling yard. The branch closed in 2006 but has been largely mothballed as there may be opencast coal production in the future.

Fig. 122 is a somewhat agricultural view of the box, still with the old suffix of Junction in the name, which it did not have at the survey date in 2008. The box has its frame facing the rear of the box and the instrument shelf above that. It used British Railways standard block instruments to communicate with

Fig. 123   Elmton and Creswell Junction wooden post home and distant signals, June 2008.

Worksop and Shirebrook Junction. The box was switched out in September 2013.

Fig. 123 is a rare view of a home and distant signal on one wooden post. The signals are guarding the route towards Shirebrook Junction.

The reopened Creswell station is shown in Fig. 124 with the platform starter for Worksop. The post or doll with the branch towards Staveley is armless, as the branch had been disconnected from the running lines by then.

Fig. 124   Reopened Elmton and Creswell station with bracket signal, June 2008.

Fig. 125 Elmton and Creswell Junction signal box – the former junction is in the undergrowth, June 2008.

Fig. 125 is a mini photo of the box; the erstwhile branch remains in the foreground.

Shirebrook Junction (SJ)

Date Built	c.1899
MR Type or Builder	Midland Type 2b+
No. of Levers	40
Way of Working	AB
Current Status	Active
Listed (Y/N)	N

Shirebrook Junction is right in the heart of what was the East Midlands coalfield.

To the north the junction is single lead but then goes to double track. Beside the double-track section is a yard of seven sidings for merry-go-round trains to power stations. Coal has to be first pulverized into a dust before use. It is transported from the disposal sites, where the pulverizing takes place, to the power station.

South of the box the junction leads off to the right, double track this time to meet up with the lines above. The amalgamated line then runs to Clipstone Junction and by the remains of the Welbeck colliery junction. Clipstone is another triangular junction but that is another story, as it is Great Central Railway territory.

Shirebrook Junction signal box is shown in Fig. 126, with the double track south leading off to the right. The rusty point almost opposite the south junction is a line to the W.H. Davis wagon works and formerly it led off to Langwith Junction – another junction surrounded by coal mines but Great Central Railway (originally Lancashire, Derbyshire and East Coast Railway) this time. The up main line of the south junction, which is the left hand of the two running lines, has catch points to derail a runaway wagon. They are usually spring-loaded. The diamond crossing is switched for the main line.

Fig. 127 shows the rear of Shirebrook Junction signal box with its many windows. The south junction to Clipstone Junction runs behind the box. Note the period stencil 15mph speed restriction sign for the junction. Nowadays the sign is a

Fig. 126 Shirebrook Junction signal box, and junction, June 2006.

Fig. 127 Rear of Shirebrook Junction signal box, June 2006.

roundel and there is always a pointer to which line the restriction refers to if there is more than one running line.

The period Midland Railway station building is shown in Fig. 128. The building beyond the left-hand platform and radio mast is the former locomotive depot, and the siding opposite that is the down refuge siding. Shirebrook had both locomotive and wagon facilities. The box is 145 miles 14 chains (233.6km) from St Pancras via Leicester and Toton.

Fig. 128   Shirebrook station and former engine shed, June 2006.

Pinxton

Date Built	1897
MR Type or Builder	Midland Type 2b
No. of Levers	28
Way of Working	AB
Current Status	Preserved Barrow Hill
Listed (Y/N)	N

Pinxton is a former mining village on the very edge of Derbyshire whose origins go back to the Domesday Book and medieval times. Coal was mined here from the eighteenth century and the Cromford Canal was an early conduit for the mines' output.

Pinxton signal box, in Fig. 129, survived so long due to its coal mining uses as well as its role supervising a road crossing at Pinxton and one at Upper Portland nearby. The box was built taller than most, no doubt to enhance the view of the severe curvature of the line back towards Shirebrook Junction. The box had only a few months to go in active service but retains its vintage name plate and overall look of a Victorian structure built in the year of Her Majesty Queen Victoria's diamond jubilee.

Fig. 130 shows Pinxton signal box crossing looking towards Shirebrook Junction. The trailing

Fig. 129   Pinxton signal box, June 2006.

Fig. 130   Pinxton with colliery access sidings and crossover, June 2006.

Fig. 131   Rear of Pinxton signal box and crossing, June 2006.

crossover and the siding signalled off the down main line on the left is to service Bentinck colliery. The siding continues on to the colliery, and the spur that results in buffer stops to the extreme left of the picture is a locomotive siding. This presumably enabled a main line locomotive to be held there whilst a colliery locomotive actually dealt with trains within the pit area. This strategically placed facility was no doubt handy for cups of tea in the box while the main line crew were waiting. The signal apparently above the 20mph speed sign is the colliery starter. All this is now plain lined with no points in the layout.

Fig. 131 shows the box from the rear, with plenty of lookout back down the road.

The signal we caught a glimpse of in Fig. 130 is a conventional home signal but also has a colour light signal on the same post. Note also that there are front and rear ladders. Sleight's East signal box is less than a mile away.

Sleight's Sidings East

Date Built	1897
MR Type or Builder	Midland Type 2a
No. of Levers	IFS
Way of Working	AB, TCB to Trent Power Box
Current Status	Preserved Embsay and Bolton Abbey Railway
Listed (Y/N)	N

Sleight's Sidings East controlled only a few colour light signals and a set of barriers for the crossing. The box was fitted with individual function switches to control it all in 1980.

The signaller must have had a bit of time to cultivate the hanging baskets although the box was a block post and would have had to handle all trains passing the box.

The box was taken out of use and control passed to Derby control centre in 2007. It was then saved

Fig. 132   Sleight's East signal box, June 2006.

Fig. 133   Rear of Sleight's East signal box, June 2006.

by a local scrap dealer and placed on their land just by where the box originally was.

The Embsay and Bolton Abbey Railway near Skipton in North Yorkshire then bought the box, dismantled it and transported it north. They hope to reassemble it and use it as a demonstration and educational resource at Bolton Abbey station.

Sleight's Sidings East is seen from the rear in Fig. 133. As there is no frame in the box there is no need for locking frame room windows. Apart from that the box looks to be in good condition despite only having a few months left to serve.

After Sleight's East the line joins up with the Erewash Valley line from Chesterfield and then proceeds towards Toton Yard as quadruple track.

Stanton Gate Shunt Frame

Date Built	1969
MR Type or Builder	BR Type LMR 15c
No. of Levers	50
Ways of Working	Shunt frame only
Current Status	Demolished 2007
Listed (Y/N)	N

Stanton Gate Shunt Frame was located on the up side of the main line from Trent Junction and was built to service the Stanton and Staveley pipe works at Ilkeston. There was a series of crossovers or a 'ladder' to reach the pipe works itself, which was on the down side. The pipe-making process involved smelting iron.

There was a smaller yard on the down side and that seems to have been for finished pipe product trains. Stanton Gate handled large quantities of iron ore, limestone and coal as raw materials. The company was eventually taken over by Saint-Gobain, the French glass manufacturer mentioned under Kirkby Thore above. They have submitted a planning application to redevelop the entire site with light industrial and housing units.

The London Midland Region box is seen in its death throes in Fig. 134, and the only question for the Network Rail team is: are they there to check for Banksy-type street art or are they there to administer the last rites?

Fig. 135 shows the shunt frame. The layout here consisted of five running tracks and the yard had six loops and a headshunt. A tandem or three-way point can be seen in the undergrowth by the box and it is easy to see from here how much space was saved using this device.

Fig. 134 *Stanton Gate Shunt Frame signal box, February 2007.*

Fig. 135 *Stanton Gate Shunt Frame signal box and track layout, February 2007.*

Fig. 136   Stapleford and Sandiacre shunt frame signal box, with Toton Yard beyond the road bridge, February 2007.

Fig. 137   Toton Yard with the DB Schenker depot across the tracks, November 2014.

Stapleford and Sandiacre

Date Built	1949
MR Type or Builder	BR Type LMR 14
No. of Levers	115
Ways of Working	Shunt frame only
Current Status	Closed 2009
Listed (Y/N)	N

Stapleford and Sandiacre was of wartime ARP (Air Raid Precautions) design with the characteristic flat roof of solid concrete from the drawing board of the LMS, although the box was recorded as being London Midland Region of BR.

At 115 levers this was a considerable piece of signalling, although the number of active levers was much reduced towards the end. A signaller reports a night shift as having about ten trains a night whereas in coal industry days there would be upwards of 100 trains. Fig. 136 is the general view of the box.

Class 60 anyone? Fig. 137 shows Toton Yard and a number of stored class 60 locomotives. The depot over the tracks is Deutsche Bahn (DB) Schenker's and there are class 08, 60 and 66 and 67s on view. On the right is a class 66 with its lights on shunting permanent way wagons of concrete sleepers and coal hoppers.

Sneinton Crossing Shunt Frame

Date Built	1914
MR Type or Builder	Midland Type 4c
No. of Levers	10
Way of Working	Gate box only
Current Status	Moved for preservation 2013
Listed (Y/N)	N

Fig. 138   Sneinton Crossing shunt frame signal box, February 2007.

Fig. 139   Side and rear view of Sneinton Crossing shunt frame signal box, February 2007.

Sneinton Crossing shunt frame was about half a mile from Nottingham Midland station and was living on borrowed time for the latter part of its operational existence. Originally there was a size-able road crossing with four barriers to look after, but later it was reduced to footpath and cycle use only. The signalling in the area is TCB from Trent power box but Sneinton was interlocked with the power box to the extent that signals for the running lines could not be pulled off, in the vicinity of the box, until the barriers had been lowered by the sig-naller. The box supervised two other crossings at Trent Lane and Colwick Road by CCTV.

The signal box succumbed in 2013 and was removed for possible preservation at the Network Rail Innovation Centre near the former Thoresby colliery, an offshoot from the Shirebrook Junction branch described above. The situation is now in a state of flux due to policy changes at the NRIC.

Burton upon Trent to Leicester

Still in the intensively coal-mined area of the East Midlands, Burton upon Trent could at least offer to slake the miners' thirst as it was and is a centre of the beer-brewing industry. In addition to coal there are copious quantities of stone, usually for road construction.

The Leicester and Swannington Railway was one of the earliest railways in England and was opened in 1832. Its purpose was to bring coal from the Leicestershire coalfield to Leicester.

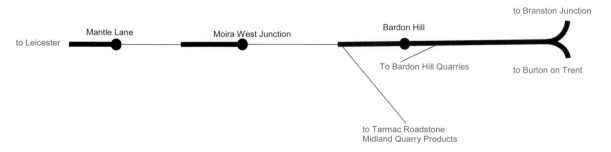

Fig. 140   Burton upon Trent to Leicester schematic diagram.

Bardon Hill (BH)

Date Built	1899
MR Type or Builder	Midland Type 2b
No. of Levers	IFS Panel
Way of Working	TCB, AB
Current Status	Active
Listed (Y/N)	N

Bardon Hill is the highest point in Leicestershire and the site of an extinct volcano. More pertinent to railway activity is that it has had a quarry here since the seventeenth century. Aggregate Industries still quarry there and massive amounts of granite stone are moved using class 66 locos and hopper wagons. The quarry produces 3 million tonnes of stone per year, and given the current rate of production, the quarry will be exhausted in 2019. However, Aggregate Industries has requested planning permission to treble the size of the workings.

The signal box at Bardon Hill was being refurbished at the time of the survey in 2008. The update included new windows and a repaint. The way of working is from individual function switches after the sixteen-lever frame was removed from the box. The box controls the line from Bagworth Junction, about 1¼ miles (2km) from the box to a point about half a mile (800m) from the Bardon Hill quarry junction, as well as the quarry connection. The box works AB to Mantle Lane in Coalville and TCB to Leicester power box. It also controls the road crossing.

Fig. 142 shows some more of the work being done at Bardon Hill but also a glimpse at the Bardon Hill quarry reception siding known as 'Front Road' and a loaded stone train ready to go. The class 66 is typical motive power.

Bardon Hill signal box is 111 miles 23 chains (179.1km) from St Pancras.

Mantle Lane (ML)

Date Built	1910
MR Type or Builder	Midland Type 4c+
No. of Levers	28, IFS panel
Way of Working	AB
Current Status	Active
Listed (Y/N)	N

Coalville was largely a creation of the Industrial Revolution and its appetite for coal, although surface coal had been garnered by villagers since medieval times. Deep coal mining was pioneered in the area and two collieries were prominent in this, Whitwick in 1824 and Snibston in 1831. George Stephenson was a key figure in these works as well as building the Leicester and Swannington railway.

Fig. 141   Bardon Hill signal box with the builders in, February 2008.

Fig. 142   Bardon Hill signal box with the builders in and a class 66 with stone train, February 2008.

Coal mining ceased at Coalville in the 1980s so the sidings that remained were a legacy of the mines, used to store stone wagons and coaches.

Snibston colliery was turned into a discovery park after closure and has many railway-related structures and artefacts as well as track work.

Fig. 143 shows Mantle Lane signal box amongst its sidings and yard. Work continues at night and the floodlights are in evidence. They seem to have signal ladders and hoops. The box also supervises crossings at Coalville station and Swannington, which is just under a mile (1.5km) away towards Leicester.

Mantle Lane signalling (Fig. 144) has the down starter and a subsidiary signal for the reception loop. There is still a pair of ground discs as a mechanical presence and keeping them company is a manual point lever.

Fig. 145 shows the side of Mantle Lane signal box with rear-mounted steps and a rake of coaches on this freight-only line. The rules would not permit any passengers to be present as there would be no facing-point locks or other passenger safety requisites on such a line.

Mantle Lane is 113 miles 5 chains (182km) from St Pancras.

Moira West Junction (MW)

Date Built	1896
MR Type or Builder	Midland Type 2b+
No. of Levers	Nx Panel
Way of Working	TCB, AB
Current Status	Active
Listed (Y/N)	N

Moira West Junction was so named after an unlikely collaboration between the Midland Railway and the London and North Western Railway. The branch ran 29 miles (47km) from the junction to Nuneaton and passed through Market Bosworth and Shackerstone, where another junction was made to Coalville. The line closed in 1970 but the Battlefield Line, with its headquarters at Shackerstone, is putting some of it back.

Fig. 143   Mantle Lane signal box, February 2008.

Fig. 144   Mantle Lane signals, October 2006.

Fig. 145   Rear and side of Mantle Lane signal box, October 2006.

Fig. 146   Moira West signal box, February 2008.

Moira West Junction signal box looks somewhat beleaguered in Fig. 164 with the mesh grilles over the windows. The box controls the line from just after Swannington crossing, which is about 5 miles (8km) from the box in the Coalville direction, to just before Gresley tunnel, which is just over half a mile from the box in the Leicester direction. In the middle of the section is the Lounge disposal point, a former opencast coal site that has received planning permission for a rail freight distribution centre. After that is the Hick Road siding owned by UK Coal, which now appears disused, and between the box and Gresley Tunnel is the Swains Park sidings, which also appear disused. After the Swains Park sidings control passes to Derby signalling centre.

Cheltenham Spa Area

Cheltenham Spa was first popularized by the Prince Regent – who was to become George IV – and anywhere he went society followed. The railways cemented the popularity of the town, and there were seven railway stations in and around the immediate area. The Midland Railway Lansdown station is the only one that has survived in Network Rail ownership. During World War II the town was a key bottleneck in the movement of supplies to the south coast ports for D-Day, and some of the tracks were quadrupled to deal with the traffic and signal boxes were built to control the new formations. Lansdown signal box, which was an example of this, still exists as a derelict ruin.

The town's major employer had been Smith's Industries, who made analogue instruments for aircraft worldwide. They also invented the Autoland system in the 1960s. They are still in business as a massive multinational and maintain a presence in the town. The largest employer now is the Government Communications Headquarters (GCHQ), who deal with electronic surveillance of terrorists and subversives.

Fig. 148 shows Cheltenham Lansdown station. There is another station in Cheltenham, or rather, just outside: Cheltenham Racecourse, operated by the Gloucestershire and Warwickshire Railway.

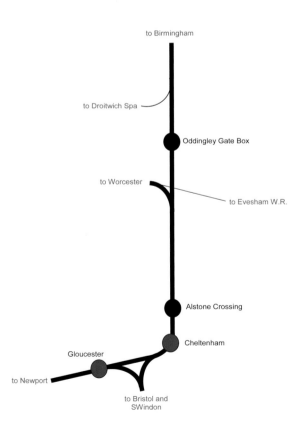

Fig. 147   Cheltenham area schematic diagram.

Fig. 148   Cheltenham station facade, September 2006.

At the end of the platform in the Birmingham direction is Alstone Crossing signal box (Fig. 149) with the additional facilities. This consists of a 'goods loop' with, unusually, a facing crossover to enable Birmingham-bound trains to access the loop. The red LED unit is the more modern version of the ground disc.

Alstone Crossing

Date Built	1891
MR Type or Builder	Midland Type 2a
No. of Levers	IFS panel
Way of Working	Gate
Current Status	Active
Listed (Y/N)	N

Fig. 149   Cheltenham station platform looking towards Birmingham, September 2006.

Alstone Crossing is officially classified as a gate box but it has the additional responsibility of issuing and collecting the one train staff for the Sharpness Branch in Gloucestershire. This means that the nuclear flask trains from Berkeley power

Fig. 150   Alstone Crossing signal box, September 2006.

station pass through here. The operator is Direct Rail Services. OTS is a means of working a single line where the issue of the staff is the authority to proceed, and no other staff can be issued subsequently except in very exceptional circumstances to rescue a broken-down train in the section. The goods loop would be able to accommodate the nuclear flask trains but not modern block trains.

Oddingley

Date Built	1908
MR Type or Builder	Midland Type 3a
No. of Levers	Annett's Key release
Way of Working	Gate
Current Status	Active
Listed (Y/N)	N

Oddingley (Fig. 151) is about as simple as a box gets but has still been built with care and is most definitely Midland Railway. Care has been taken with the slate roof with lead flashing and finial, and the staircase is a Lilliputian delight. There is no lever frame here but there is a device called an Annett's Key, which is basically an interlocking device. The gates are normally closed across the road, the opposite of normal, but if no train is approaching the signaller may remove the key and open the gates.

Fig. 151   Oddingley signal box, June 2012.

If the key is removed and a train is approaching, the signals are turned to danger automatically.

Fig. 152 is Oddingley gate box looking towards Birmingham.

Chinley Junction to Buxton

This short line has only two boxes on it and yet has a volume of freight traffic not seen on many other lines on Network Rail, based on stone and cement traffic. This traffic runs through craggy Peak District scenery.

Fig. 152   Oddingley signal box looking towards Birmingham, June 2012.

Peak Forest South

Date Built	1925
MR Type or Builder	Midland Type 4d
No. of Levers	50
Way of Working	AB
Current Status	Active
Listed (Y/N)	N

There is no station at Peak Forest South now but there is a DB Schenker locomotive depot, where drivers can sign on and locomotives can be refuelled. This is unusual these days and is a measure of the traffic still operated on this line.

Fig. 154 shows that Peak Forest South signal box is very much a functional working box that does not seem very concerned with its appearance. It is another Midland design perpetuated by the LMS after amalgamation. The windows are just to look out of and have no decorative merit or sympathy with the box's origins. The class 60 in the background is accompanied by a class 66 next to it. They are very much the mainstay of traction here and, following DB Schenker's announcement in September 2014 that the 08 shunter locos were to be retired or sold off, class 66s can be seen shunting the layout.

Fig. 155 shows the track configuration at Peak Forest South looking towards Great Rocks Junction. On the left a class 66 is shunting the train but this loco will not be the train engine; both signal posts on the left refer to the main running line so all signals are on. Then there are the two running lines past the box front heading for Chinley Junction toward the camera. Behind the box are locomotive stabling sidings and wagon storage sidings, probably for crippled wagons, where the class 60 is; and finally, nearest the camera, is the refuelling point, where there is another class 66. There are also basic servicing facilities with bogie-level floodlights and a concrete pan instead of sleepers.

Looking the other way at Peak Forest South, towards Chinley Junction, there are stone quarrying and crushing facilities. The stone trains are made up here and the company's blue shunter is

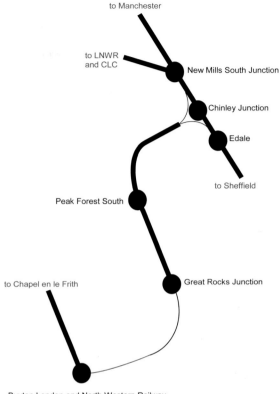

Fig. 153   Chinley Junction–Buxton schematic diagram.

Fig. 154   Peak Forest South signal box, October 2014.

Fig. 155   Peak Forest South signal box, yards and loco depot, October 2014.

Fig. 156   Cemex yard looking towards Chinley Junction, October 2014.

Fig. 157   Peak Forest South signal box, yards and detail, October 2014.

Fig. 158   Peak Forest yard from Great Rocks Junction, October 2014.

hiding quite effectively on the extreme right of Fig. 156. The company RMC was formerly Ready Mixed Concrete Ltd and now Cemex.

More detail of the yard is visible in Fig. 157, and interestingly there is no trap point on the goods loop in front of the box, as this is a freight-only line now. Note that there is a red-and-white chequered Limited Clearance plate on the end of the box.

The difference between the 1960s tubular post signal in the foreground and the galvanized steel bracket signal is quite striking. The limit of shunt indicator for the company's shunter is a bespoke one for the location, just at the bottom of the home and distant signal post. It reads 'Limit of Shunt for Cemex Staff'.

Behind the aforementioned post is a single slip.

Fig. 159   Peak Forest yard overview, August 2006.

Fig. 160   Peak Forest and DB Schenker loco yard and former station, October 2014.

Fig. 158 shows the same class 66 that was doing the shunting in Fig. 155 except that we are looking at it with Great Rocks Junction behind the camera and Peak Forest South in front. The class 60 is also the same one as in that photo.

Most of the layout at Peak Forest South is on display in Fig. 159. One stone train is ready to receive a loco to come back towards the camera and Chinley Junction. This view is eight years earlier than the others but not much has changed.

Fig. 160 shows the DB Schenker loco depot with a customer at the former passenger station building. Note that whitewash has been used to make sighting the home signal easier, on the right by the bridge.

Great Rocks Junction

Date Built	1923
MR Type or Builder	Midland Type 4d+
No. of Levers	34
Way of Working	AB, KT
Current Status	Active
Listed (Y/N)	N

Fig. 161   Great Rocks Junction signal box, October 2014.

Fig. 162   Great Rocks Junction and Tunstead Works, with the single track to Buxton on the far left, October 2014.

Fig. 163   Great Rocks Junction and subsidiary signals controlling entry and exit to Tunstead Works, October 2014.

Fig. 164   Great Rocks Junction, Tunstead Works and a class 66 preparing to leave with a cement train, October 2014.

Great Rocks Junction signal box looks more like a BR LMR box after it was rebuilt with a flat roof (Fig. 161); it was also refurbished in 2004.

The box works AB to Peak Forest South and key token to Buxton LNWR signal box. Key token is used on single lines and consists of a token instrument in each signal box. When a token is withdrawn from one box and issued to a driver to carry forward, the box at the other end is mechanically locked and no further token can be issued until the original one is placed in the box at the other end. This locking of the instruments also inhibits pulling off signals or giving Line Clear to admit another train onto a single line. There are usually several tokens in the instruments, as you may be in the situation where a few trains travel in the same direction before any return in the opposite direction.

Fig. 162 shows Great Rocks Junction and the view looking towards the single track to Buxton, which is on the extreme left. There are a total of six

Fig. 165   Tunstead Works and a class 66 preparing to enter the main line, October 2014.

Fig. 166   Class 66 on its way to Peak Forest South, October 2014.

subsidiary armed signals to marshal traffic in and out of the cement workings, known as Tunstead Works. There is also a train that has been prepared for a main line diesel by a works shunter, which is stabled by the cement tankers. There are three works shunters in about a mile of running track so this place is busy. The single-line token for trains to Buxton would normally be exchanged at the box manually.

Fig. 163 shows Great Rocks Junction signal box further up from the cement works. There are another five signals to control the sidings.

Fig. 164 and the following pictures track a cement train from the time the loco backs onto the train until it leaves Great Rocks Junction section and heads for Peak Forest South. The class 66 is ready to leave and the 'board', or arm, is off ready for it. The larger post in the foreground is for the single-track Buxton branch.

The train is making its way towards Great Rocks Junction signal box in Fig. 165 and onto the main running line toward Peak Forest South.

In Fig. 166 the train has passed Great Rocks Junction box, gone underneath the road overbridge and is now on the up running line heading towards Peak Forest South, where the class 60 is further up the line.

Leeds to Sheffield

The line between these two cities of half a million people each generated massive volumes of coal and steel traffic, and there were huge complexes of goods yards, loco sheds and signal boxes as well as passenger stations. The very much simplified diagram in Fig. 167 represents what is left of that infrastructure. The diagram also takes no account of line ownership, as the position is extremely complicated. The Great Northern, Great Central as well as the North Eastern and Lancashire and Yorkshire were around this area.

The Midland Railway main line, however, ran from St Pancras to Leicester, Nottingham and Sheffield. From there the line went to Leeds,

Skipton, Settle and Carlisle. The Midland did get to York and it had a large engine shed there, but that was over joint metals with the North Eastern Railway.

Moorthorpe (M)

Date Built	1908
MR Type or Builder	Midland Type 4c+
No. of Levers	36
Way of Working	TCB
Current Status	Demolished 2011
Listed (Y/N)	N

Moorthorpe signal box was a victim of its usefulness in the sense that the loops were seen to be very useful to shunt freights into whilst passenger trains overtook them. The fact that the signalling was seen to be at the end of its life led to the demolition of both this box and Hickleton, and the replacement with more modern equipment. The budget was, apparently, £16 million.

Of course the fact that the equipment is relatively modern is a testimony to the durability of the colour light signalling systems that replaced the semaphore signalling in the first place, but times change and technology moves faster than the expectations of permanence.

The view in Fig. 168 is to the front. The windows had been largely boarded up by the time of the

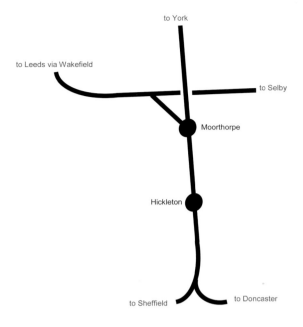

Fig. 167   Leeds–Sheffield schematic diagram.

survey. The lever frame only operated switches to operate signals and points: there was no mechanical signalling here.

Moorthorpe signal box is depicted again in Fig. 169, and here the goods loops are clearly shown. There was also a connection to Frickley colliery but that connection has been removed. The station is just beyond the loops.

Fig. 168   Moorthorpe signal box, April 2010.

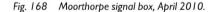

Fig. 169   Moorthorpe signal box, partial side view and goods loops, April 2010.

Fig. 170   Hickleton signal box, April 2010.

Hickleton (H)

Date Built	1931
MR Type or Builder	LMS Type 11b+
No. of Levers	50
Way of Working	TCB
Current Status	Demolished 2011
Listed (Y/N)	N

Hickleton signal box served the coal industry in the area where Hickleton Main colliery shaft was first sunk in 1894. When the colliery closed there were said to be 3sq miles (8sq km) of workings underneath the mine shaft. Hickleton had been 'Hickleton Main Colliery' signal box.

The box, in Fig. 170, is in a world of its own, as all the sidings and other infrastructure around a colliery have disappeared. The area was freshly landscaped at the time of the survey and it needed a dash of imagination to realize there had been a major industrial undertaking in the area. According to the legend on the cabinet outside, Hickleton was 15 miles 4 chains (24.2km) from Burton Salmon junction, in the general direction of York.

CHAPTER 3

Lancashire and Yorkshire Railway

Unlike the Midland Railway, the Lancashire and Yorkshire Railway did what it said on the tin and kept to those boundaries mostly, that is to say the pre-1974 local government reorganization picture of the two counties. Liverpool and Manchester and the surrounds were part of Lancashire then.

There was a brief foray into Lincolnshire with the Axholme Joint Railway together with the North Eastern Railway, but this was the summit of its excursions.

It was a intensive network that linked many of the northern cities except Leeds. The actual route mileages were short and the total was only about 600 miles (1,000km) but from that were worked extremely intensive services. It had 738 signal boxes, some jointly owned. It also owned thirty ships, more than any other railway company.

The Lancashire and Yorkshire eventually wound up with 1,650 locomotives, which ran 24.4 million miles (39.3 million km) in 1919. There were fifty-seven pages of Bradshaw's railway time-table devoted to the L&Y although no two stations were more than 5½ miles (9km) apart. The longest non-stop run was Manchester to Wakefield at 47¾ miles (76.8km) but it ran dining cars on all its top expresses.

Manchester Victoria was its principal station, with seventeen platforms that handled 700 trains a day in 1912. Like the other railways, the main source of income was the movement of coal, and the L&Y had a hand in the lucrative export of coal from the Yorkshire coalfield from the port of Goole. At the other end of the network, at its peak, the L&Y marshalled 2 million tons of coal per year into its yards at Aintree, Liverpool, either for export or for bunkering ships at Liverpool docks.

The scene was very different in recent times, with most of the major cities being modernized with track circuit block and multiple aspect signals (MAS) from the 1960s on. However, L&Y territory mechanical signalling has survived in pockets and the absolute epicentre of it now is Blackpool North station. There is the preserved East Lancashire Railway, which is virtually all mechanically signalled, and there are L&Y signalling artefacts at Llanuwchllyn Station on the Bala Lake Railway outside the ex-GWR signal box. One of the Bala Lake pioneers was an L&Y signaller.

There is also the L&Y signalling school model railway at the National Railway Museum.

The pace of change is accelerating, thanks to extensions to the Manchester Metro and the Liverpool–Manchester electrification.

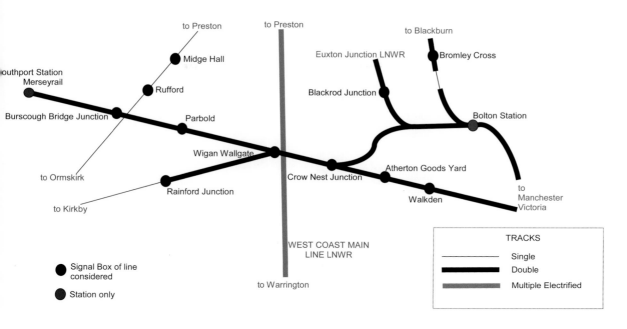

Fig. 171   West Lancashire schematic diagram.

West Lancashire

Fig. 171 is a simplified schematic that shows West Lancashire mostly in an L&Y context, for the sake of clarity. Furthermore, to present a coherent picture over a relatively small area the signal boxes of several lines are shown together.

A good many of the railway's express trains originated from Southport, which was and is the home of many wealthy businesspeople. In addition, further north, the resorts of Blackpool and Lytham St Annes also had their own express trains.

Southport is a splendid station and, unlike many other seaside termini, has no mechanical signalling left, partly as it is now controlled by Merseyrail.

The route we shall take will be from Southport to Manchester Victoria, Ormskirk to Preston and then the other boxes. Note that some of the boxes

subsequently closed after the survey date and the ways of working have consequently changed.

Burscough Bridge Junction (BB)

Date Built	1922
LYR Type or Builder	L&Y+
No. of Levers	IFS Panel
Way of Working	AB
Current Status	Active
Listed (Y/N)	N

Fig. 172   Burscough Bridge Junction signal box, February 2006.

Fig. 173   Burscough Bridge station, February 2006.

Fig. 174   Parbold signal box, February 2006.

Burscough Bridge Junction signal box (Fig. 172) has a projected life until 2019. The line is not a junction any more; the line from Preston to Ormskirk passes close by but they are not connected though there is talk of re-establishing the link. The box was mechanical up until 1993 when the IFS panel was installed. To the right is the Southport direction and the left Wigan and Manchester.

Burscough Bridge Junction station, shown in Fig. 173, owes something to the Midland Gothic parish church style of architecture.

The prominent bay window at the front of the building was sometimes where the very early signalling equipment was kept, and this was partly because the signaller might be tasked with collection and issue of tickets and parcels handling between signalling duties.

Accidents and mishaps over the formative years of the railway system led to recommendations that railway companies established separate buildings and posts for signallers and that they should not be engaged in general railway matters.

The modern buildings on the left, over the tracks, are where the extensive goods yard was. As this was an interchange station, there would be much re-marshalling of goods trains here. Bricked-up locking frame room windows usually indicate a box that has been in the wars – literally.

The box is 27 miles and 50 chains (44.5km) from Manchester Victoria station.

Parbold (PB)

Date Built	1877
LYR Type or Builder	Saxby & Farmer Type 9 (L&Y)
No. of Levers	20
Way of Working	AB
Current Status	Active
Listed (Y/N)	Y

Parbold signal box – or cabin, as it styles itself – is in splendid condition and is from the stable of Saxby & Farmer, one of the oldest and most revered of makers. In fact the French word for semaphore railway signal was 'le saxby', such was the company's fame in the early years of railway signalling.

The chalet style with the overhanging roof and intricate wood supports is most noteworthy, and many Continental boxes have a similar outline. A good deal of the box was rebuilt in 1983 when the top half collapsed when the original frame was removed.

Fig. 175 shows Parbold signal box looking towards Wigan, and there are semaphore signals. The distant signal is a little unusual as the next box

Fig. 175   Parbold signal box looking towards Wigan Wallgate, February 2006.

Fig. 176   Parbold signal box side and rear view, February 2006.

is Wigan Wallgate, which is over 9 miles (14km) away. It may be that the distant is motorized and controlled from Wigan. The combined home and distant signal can also be there if the stopping distance provided by the conventional distant signal is thought to be inadequate. This then gives an additional layer of warning but the distant signal must be interlocked so that it cannot be pulled off if the home signal and inner distant are at danger, or on.

The side and rear of Parbold signal box are shown in Fig. 176. The window enables reconnaissance of the traffic situation and the rearward-facing steps are a feature.

The box is 24 miles and 49 chains (39.6km) from Manchester Victoria station.

Wigan Wallgate (WW)

Date Built	1941
LYR Type or Builder	LMS Type 13
No. of Levers	Nx Panel
Way of Working	AB, TCB
Current Status	Active
Listed (Y/N)	N

Wigan Wallgate signal box is of the utilitarian ARP type that was designed to be somewhat proof against bomb-blast damage. The roofs are slabs of reinforced concrete and they usually forgo locking room frame windows, as all the others considered to be at risk during World War II were bricked up.

The box sits at the junction of the lines to Kirkby via Rainford Junction and Southport. Wigan Wallgate station is past the green colour light signal on the right-hand side of the box in Fig. 177.

Fig. 177   Wigan Wallgate signal box, November 2014.

Fig. 178   Wigan Wallgate station and off repeater, February 2006.

Fig. 179   Wigan Wallgate station and corresponding signal, February 2006.

The lines then run through Wigan Wallgate station and emerge the other side for Manchester Victoria. There is a connecting line and a pair of exchange sidings for Wigan North Western, which is the ex-LNWR station on the West Coast Main Line. In common with many L&Y stations, Wallgate has a single bay platform with an island platform for the main running lines. Opposite the box there are three sidings on the Southport side.

The massive concrete name board, applied to both sides of the box, must be a post-war addition, as all such clues to where things were had to be removed at the outbreak of war. This, coupled with the blackout, made travelling after dark a real challenge.

Wigan Wallgate worked AB to Parbold and Rainford Junction and TCB to Crow Nest Junction, in the Manchester direction. The signal box is 18 miles and 9 chains (29.1km) from Manchester Victoria.

Fig. 178 shows Wigan Wallgate station with a train waiting to leave for Southport. The bay platform referred to above is just to the right of the class 156 DMU. There is a caption indicator just by the clock that states 'OFF'; this refers to the status of the platform starter and is a repeater to inform the guard, who used to be in the charge of the train, whether it is safe to give the signal to depart, used because of longer trains and a curved platform. Off means that the signal is green or go.

Wigan Wallgate station and the signal that the guard couldn't directly see is off (Fig. 179). The feather, or branch, on top of the signal would be lit if the train was going to Rainford and Kirkby, but Southport is considered to be straight on.

Finally at Wigan Wallgate, in Fig. 180 a class 142 is arriving at the station from Southport past Wigan Wallgate signal box behind the bridge that carries the West Coast Main Line. This view of the box is from the rear.

Fig. 180   Class 142 making its way past Wigan Wallgate signal box for the station platform, WCML above, November 2014.

Crow Nest Junction (CN)

Date Built	1972
LYR Type or Builder	BR LMR Type 15
No. of Levers	25
Way of Working	AB, TCB
Current Status	Demolished 2013
Listed (Y/N)	N

Crow Nest Junction signal box (Fig. 181) controlled the double junction off the Wigan Manchester line that connected with Lostock Junction and Bolton. This route is a parallel way to access Manchester Victoria. The junctions with the line to Blackburn and Euxton Junction are all trailing in the Manchester direction so any journey via Wigan Wallgate would require reversal at Bolton.

The ways of working were: absolute block to Atherton Goods Yard and Manchester, although Atherton was switched out evenings and weekends; track circuit block to Wigan Wallgate and Bolton to Manchester Piccadilly signalling centre. The box was located near Hindley on the outskirts of Greater Manchester, 18 miles and 9 chains (29.1km) from Manchester Victoria.

Fig. 182 is a clearer view of the lines described.

Atherton Goods Yard

Date Built	1956
LYR Type or Builder	BR LMR Type 15
No. of Levers	25
Way of Working	AB
Current Status	Demolished 2013
Listed (Y/N)	N

Atherton Goods Yard signal box in later years had no goods yard but these names have a habit of lingering on after the original purpose has changed. The box depicted in Fig. 183 is almost a carbon copy of Crow Nest Junction although it was built sixteen years earlier.

The sole purpose of the box, in later years, was to provide another block post in which a train could be accommodated when the line was busy. When

Fig. 181 Crow Nest Junction signal box, August 2006.

Fig. 182 Crow Nest Junction signal box and the double-track junction, August 2006.

Fig. 183 Atherton Goods Yard signal box, February 2006.

Fig. 184   Atherton Goods Yard signal box with the station in the foreground, February 2006.

Walkden (WN)

Date Built	1888
LYR Type or Builder	Railway Signalling Company (L&Y)
No. of Levers	24
Way of Working	AB
Current Status	Demolished 2013
Listed (Y/N)	N

the line was not busy the box could be switched out. This means that all its functions would be bypassed and all signals would be off, giving trains a straight run through until they got to the next section. On double lines, switching out of a straight double track is no problem to the interlocking but on single lines a special lever must be provided to cancel the locking before all signals can be pulled off, as there would be conflicting movements signalled normally. There is an example of this at Lugton on the Glasgow and South Western Railway (*see* Chapter 5). The goods yard from which the box derived its name was located where the warehouse is on the same side and beyond. The view is looking towards Wigan Wallgate. At the time of its demise the box only had five working levers.

The box was 11 miles and 18 chains (18.1km) from Manchester Victoria.

Atherton station is shown in Fig. 184 looking towards Wigan again, with the L&Y decoration in the cast iron. The line was quadruple track through here when the signal box was built in the 1950s but it closed in 1999. The delays were found to be unacceptable so the box was reopened in 2001 during weekdays. When traffic really started to increase a few years later, however, it had to go.

Walkden signal box (Fig. 185) operated from the original quadruple track formation in 1888 to 2013, a matter of 125 years. The Railway Signalling Company of Liverpool built signal boxes for other railways, notably the Great Central, which became part of the LNER. As with Atherton, the formation was reduced to double track in later years. There was a trailing crossover here just in front of the box, and the box in the end had seven working levers.

Walkden station is elevated – in contrast to Atherton, which is in a cutting. However, there is the typical island platform and the L&Y canopies look tidy in Fig. 186. The quadruple tracks were removed from here in November 1965. Where there is quadruple track the absolute block instruments have to be doubled up, as one set is required for each pair of running lines.

Fig. 185   Walkden signal box, February 2006.

Fig. 186   Walkden, a typical L&Y station, February 2006.

Walton Junction to Preston

Rufford (RD)

Date Built	1988
LYR Type or Builder	Portakabin
No. of Levers	IFS Panel
Way of Working	KT, OTS
Current Status	Active
Listed (Y/N)	N

Rufford Old Hall is a fine Tudor house dating back 500 years and the ancestral home of the Hesketh family, who were instrumental in developing the town of Fleetwood. It is owned by the National Trust.

In L&Y days the line was an important route to the north for the company and was double track. In BR days its importance was reduced, due to other routes using former LNWR tracks and the southern end was cut back to Ormskirk. So although the bridges betray a double-track origin all the other infrastructure has changed to reflect single-line status.

The box in Fig. 187 is purely functional and lacking any aesthetic merit. This must always be a matter of personal opinion but in this case who would disagree?

The box works one train staff from Ormskirk to Rufford and then key token from Rufford to Midge Hall, near Preston. This is the only place on the line where trains can pass. The box is due to be replaced in 2017.

Fig. 187   Rufford signal box, March 2008.

Midge Hall (MH)

Date Built	1972
LYR Type or Builder	BR LMR Type 15
No. of Levers	20
Way of Working	KT
Current Status	Active
Listed (Y/N)	N

Midge Hall is quite near the crossing of Sod Hall, which seems singularly appropriate. Fig. 188 shows a box that has a crossing and nothing else. The key token apparatus is the red box with the curved top in the second window from the left. There is a semaphore signal in the Ormskirk direction and a colour light in the Preston direction.

There is a pub nearby called the Midge Hall, which is notable for its floral displays. Midge Hall signal box is 22 miles and 79 chains (37km) from the former Liverpool Exchange station.

Wigan Wallgate to Kirkby

Rainford Junction

Date Built	1933
LYR Type or Builder	LMS Type 11c
No. of Levers	10
Way of Working	AB, NSKT
Current Status	Active
Listed (Y/N)	N

Rainford Junction was a place where two double-tracked railways crossed one another. There was a line from Ormskirk that formed a junction at Rainford and then continued as LNWR to St Helens.

In Fig. 189 we can see the rear of Rainford Junction signal box, somewhat quirkily, because it has wooden trussing to hold the structure up. The current station is behind the camera and the platform used to curve around to the left. The box works AB to Wigan Wallgate and no signaller key token on the single line to Kirkby. The view is in the Kirkby direction.

The signaller has just received the key token from the driver of the class 156 DMU in Fig. 190, and the unit can now proceed to Wigan Wallgate. There is only one way of working this NSKT and there are only two tokens at this particular location. The driver of a freight train is issued with Token A to unlock the ground frame at Kirkby and lock the train in once inside the Knowsley Freight Terminal siding. After that Token B can be issued for a passenger train from the box again. The action of the driver of the freight train locking the train within the siding – so there is no chance of a collision – enables the token machine at Rainford to issue the other token to a passenger train. The no signaller designation refers to the actions of the driver at the other end of the line from the box who must use the token machine there, remotely.

Fig. 191 shows the view towards Wigan Wallgate with the class 156 disappearing into the distance.

Fig. 188   Midge Hall signal box, March 2008.

Fig. 189   Rainford Junction signal box and crutch, November 2014.

Fig. 190 Rainford Junction signal box and collecting the single-line token from the journey from Kirkby, November 2014.

Fig. 191 Rainford Junction and the class 156 well on its way to Wigan Wallgate, November 2014.

Rainford Junction station is 24 miles 30 chains (39.2km) from Manchester Victoria via Wigan, and the box another 5 chains (0.1km) more.

North of Bolton

Blackrod Junction (BJ)

Date Built	1881
LYR Type or Builder	Gloucester Wagon Co. (L&Y)
No. of Levers	37
Way of Working	TCB
Current Status	Demolished 2013
Listed (Y/N)	N

Blackrod Junction was the junction for the Horwich branch and Horwich was the locomotive works for the Lancashire and Yorkshire Railway. The works closed in 1964 for loco repairs but carried on until 1983 with mainly wagon work. The works, post-war, built LMS 2–6–0 mixed traffic, Black Five 4–6–0 and standard locos, the last in 1957. The LMS 'Crab' 2–6–0 locos were all built at Horwich.

There were three platforms and an extensive goods yard when the works were going strong.

The box in Fig. 192 is a real early oddity, and there are those who feel it was older than the recorded date suggests as the L&Y had started to build their own boxes by 1881. A more likely date is

1879. It retained the thirty-seven L&Y lever frame to the last and only had a crossover to control as well as signals.

The box survived as long as it did by a quirk of fate, in that the two signalling systems of Preston power box and Manchester Piccadilly signalling centres were not compatible – Blackrod Junction simply passed trains from one system to the other.

Bromley Cross

Date Built	1875
LYR Type or Builder	Yardley Type 1 (L&Y)
No. of Levers	16
Way of Working	Gate
Current Status	Active
Listed (Y/N)	N (under application)

Fig. 192 Blackrod Junction signal box, August 2006.

Bromley Cross had the same function as Blackrod Junction, and now those incompatibility problems have been resolved, the box simply supervises the crossing and uses an interlock with Manchester Piccadilly to control wicket gates using just four levers. The rest are painted white.

The box is depicted in Fig. 193, standing by to repel boarders. Also on view is the historic station clock, apparently more than 100 years old, and buildings that are the subject, as is the box, of a preservation attempt. Note how low the platform is here, though further on towards the Bolton end it is raised to normal height. This is usually a sign of an early installation.

Fig. 193   Bromley Cross signal box, July 2008.

Manchester to Oldham

Fig. 194 is a simplified schematic that shows the area around Manchester, as far as the L&Y went, and the 'Oldham loop'. The loop was closed in 2009 and parts of the route converted into the Oldham–Rochdale line (ORL) of the Manchester Metrolink tram system.

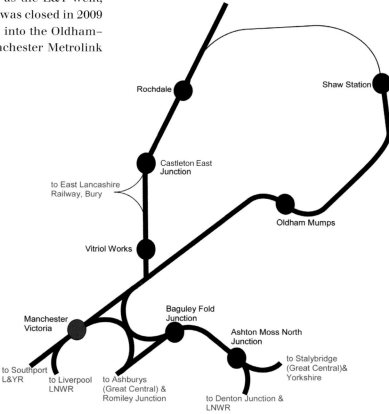

Fig. 194   Manchester–Oldham schematic diagram.

Part of the railway route survives, as it forms the route from Manchester to Bradford and Leeds, although Leeds was not a city in which the L&Y had a direct presence. Manchester to Bradford forms a separate part of this book.

The two remaining L&Y signal boxes in Manchester are included in this section. There had been a multiplicity of L&Y boxes in and around Manchester Victoria, with the carriage sidings at Miles Platting and large locomotive depots at Newton Heath and Agecroft. The station at Manchester Victoria was linked by a long platform to the LNWR Manchester Exchange station, and at 2,238ft (682m) long or getting on for half a mile, it was the longest station platform in Europe. It was used for newspaper and parcels trains as Manchester was a northern hub and originator for their distribution. The Lancashire cotton-spinning industry was once the largest in the world, and at its peak imported 2 million tons of raw cotton a year, mostly through Liverpool docks, although at the turn of the nineteenth century the Manchester Ship Canal took a share with regular sailings from Galveston in Texas. The L&Y handled this traffic up to four times before the finished products were shipped out.

Ashton Moss North Junction (AM)

Date Built	1911
LYR Type or Builder	L&Y+
No. of Levers	56
Way of Working	AB
Current Status	Active
Listed (Y/N)	N

There had been a group of sidings here built by the Great Central Railway as an interchange point for goods wagons. Hitherto wagons had to be swapped over at Penistone or Barnsley, causing a bottleneck at those busy places. This method of working continued for as long as there were wagon load freight trains – into the 1980s.

Ashton Moss North Junction signal box worked absolute block to Stalybridge box (now closed),

Fig. 195   Ashton Moss North Junction signal box, November 2014.

which is an ex-Great Central, LNER box to the east; also AB to Denton Junction in the south, which is of LNWR, LMS origin; and AB to Baguley Fold Junction, which is ex-L&Y, LMS.

The block instruments of all the various companies had to be made to work together; while they all operated on the same principles, they were quite different in their construction and engineering.

The box in Fig. 195 appears in fine fettle except for the pronounced sag in the middle!

Fig. 196 shows the double junction at Ashton Moss North Junction signal box; the tracks are split up because the box is in the middle of the junction, no doubt to afford a good view of proceedings. The lines from Denton Junction (LNWR) come in at the bottom right. The gantry before the box and the bracket after it seem to be for overhead catenary and it must be the ex-LNER 1500v DC Woodhead route, dismantled in the 1980s.

The pair of lines on the right has come from Ashton-under-Lyne station, behind the camera, and Stalybridge, which was Great Central territory. The lines then proceed up the page towards Baguley Fold Junction signal box and junction, our next stop.

Fig. 196 Ashton Moss North Junction signal box and junction layout and signalling, November 2014.

Ashton Moss North Junction signal box is 5 miles and 52 chains (9km) from Miles Platting junction near Manchester Victoria station.

The lines to Denton Junction curve away in Fig. 197, looking the other way to the previous figure. The sharp curvature is clear, and this is reinforced by the check rails on the inside of the running rails, which help to keep wheels on the track and minimize flange and track wear. The catenary posts show up well. There are no wires and pulleys going this way so no more semaphore signals either. There is plenty of electrical cable, however, with Smartwater warnings for the colour lights.

Fig. 198 is a long-range shot towards Ashton-under-Lyne station. The Oldham Road overbridge appears to have been raised as if for electrification.

Baguley Fold Junction (BF)

Date Built	1890
LYR Type or Builder	Railway Signalling Company (L&Y)
No. of Levers	IFS Panel
Way of Working	AB
Current Status	Active
Listed (Y/N)	N

Baguley Fold Junction signal box featured in an accident in 1982 when the box was supervising a crossing at Clayton Bridge, which is some ¾ miles (1.2km) from the box, and was observed by CCTV.

A DMU was travelling from Manchester Victoria to Leeds and it collided with a private car on the crossing. The driver was seriously injured and his passenger sustained a minor injury. A track circuit on the side of the crossing beyond the box had failed and as they are always fail-safe, it put the signal guarding the crossing to danger. The signaller had lowered the barriers from the box and was signalling the DMU manually in view of the track circuit failure and signal at danger. The passage of another

Fig. 197 Ashton Moss North Junction lines to Denton Junction with overhead 1500v DC catenary posts in place, November 2014.

Fig. 198 Ashton Moss North Junction towards Ashton-under-Lyne station, November 2014.

Fig. 199   Baguley Fold Junction signal box, November 2014.

Fig. 200   Baguley Fold Junction signal box with signal wire post detail, November 2014.

train on the other track caused the barriers to rise and so the driver set off, only to be hit by the three-car unit. There is no mechanical signalling any longer at Baguley Fold Junction.

The box was reinforced for World War II and the locking frame windows bricked up. The box appears to be in good condition in Fig. 199 despite the roof being covered with some fabric material instead of the usual slate. The 15mph sign outside the box refers to the speed limit for the lines round to Ardwick and Ashburys whence the connection to Romiley Junction is made (*see* Chapter 2). Straight on to the left is to Miles Platting junction and Manchester Victoria. To the right the line goes to Ashton Moss North Junction and Stalybridge and across the Pennines to Leeds.

Pulling back a bit, Fig. 200 shows the staircase on the left going down to street level and Ten Acre Lane. On the right is the start of the small posts with pulleys, which are all that is left of the semaphore signalling here. Each signal had a wire and a pulley, and there must be about twenty pulleys. The box was built with twenty-six levers originally but this was expanded when a power station nearby had sidings built for it. The power station

must have been one of the municipal types that just served the local area before the National Grid, and is long gone.

Vitriol Works (VW)

Date Built	1954
LYR Type or Builder	BR LMR Type 14
No. of Levers	65
Way of Working	AB
Current Status	Active
Listed (Y/N)	N

Vitriol Works suggests either a comment on the efficacy of abuse on social networks or a signal box that was built near a factory that manufactured sulphuric acid. Here it is the latter.

Despite its modernistic ARP appearance it contained L&Y block instruments and replaced an L&Y box a few yards up the line. Construction started in 1953 and the work was instigated by the building of Chadderton B power station nearby. The layout consisted of a group of sidings opposite the box with a headshunt, which enables any shunting to be carried out off the running lines.

Fig. 201   Vitriol Works signal box, November 2014.

Fig. 201 depicts a signal box similar to Wigan Wallgate but without the massive concrete nameplates. It is now just a block post from Manchester signalling centre on its way to Bradford over the Pennines, now that the Oldham loop is no more. The land where the power station sidings were is where the camera is. All of the surrounds have been sold off for industrial units.

Vitriol Works signal box is itself engulfed by industrial buildings – as Fig. 202 shows, it is some firm's car park. The box name plate is pure 1950s BR London Midland Region.

Finally at Vitriol Works, the rear and side view is shown in Fig. 203. At the rear of the box there was a chemical works named after its owner, Hannibal Becker, who was in business in 1848 when the line opened. Becker, a naturalized German, had operated a calico works at Reddish near Stockport and then the sulphuric acid plant. He was also productive in other areas, as he sired fifteen children.

Castleton East Junction (CE)

Date Built	1963
LYR Type or Builder	BR LMR Type 15
No. of Levers	65
Way of Working	AB
Current Status	Active
Listed (Y/N)	N

Fig. 202   Vitriol Works signal box end with LMR maroon plate, August 2006.

Castleton East Junction has had a varied past over the years. The junction was to the station at Heywood and subsequently Bury Bolton Street. This is now the main operating base of the East Lancashire Railway (ELR). Bury Bolton Street station is fully signalled; the flavour is 1950s/60s BR London Midland Region and very authentic.

In addition to the Bury line there was a branch to Bolton and connections to Bacup and Accrington in north Lancashire. There had been a steelworks

Fig. 203   Vitriol Works signal box rear and side view, August 2006.

nearby but in later years the yard at Castleton, on the down side and same side as the box, was extensive, with ten sidings and seven loops. There were five sidings on the up side, opposite the box. More recently, it had become a materials depot for railway equipment. The original survey in 2006 found most of this track work in position, although obviously much of it was disused.

Perhaps the most regular user of the line was the ELR, with regular steam locomotives going on to Bury Bolton Street, as well as classic diesels including Deltics.

At present the box is still there and it has its name plate; there are a few semaphore signals but the up yard opposite the box has gone. There is now a new Rochdale signal box that will completely take over the functions of Castleton East Junction eventually, and seemingly that process is overdue.

Fig. 204 shows the box in modern guise still with its name plate (the removal of the name plate means a box is not in use any longer). The birch trees are slowly enveloping the area where the up sidings were.

Castleton East Junction and environs in the modern era are shown in Fig. 205. Colour light signals have appeared and a new crossover in the bottom right on the picture, for the ELR no doubt. The signaller's car is still in attendance and there are semaphore signals in evidence. Behind the

Fig. 204   Castleton East Junction signal box, October 2014.

buffer stops at the far end of track there was a further access to the Heywood line, and this formed a triangle with the line in the foreground that runs past the front of the box. This was a useful facility to turn steam locomotives, as the ELR do not have a turntable. Note that all the facing ground discs are track circuited.

Fig. 206 shows Castleton East Junction from the rear and from the past (in 2006). A class 142 Pacer heads past the home and distant semaphores on its way to Manchester Victoria. Note the two signals on a bracket that control access to the station the other side of the bridge – one for the main running line and one for the exit from the yard.

Fig. 207 shows Castleton East Junction yard and some semaphores. On the right are the exit signals

Fig. 205   Castleton East Junction
signal box and layout looking towards
Manchester, October 2014.

Fig. 206   Castleton East Junction signal box and class 142 heading for Manchester, August 2006.

Fig. 207   Castleton East Junction yard signals, August 2006.

However, the Rochdale box will be relatively short-lived before everything migrates to the Manchester Rail Operating Centre.

Rochdale (RE)

Date Built	1889
LYR Type or Builder	Railway Signalling Company (L&Y)
No. of Levers	30
Way of Working	AB
Current Status	Demolished 2011
Listed (Y/N)	N

for the up sidings and the larger armed signal for the down running line. The ground disc was not track circuited at this date.

Fig. 208 shows the shape of the future on the left in the shape of Rochdale West signal box, with Castleton East Junction looking on, perhaps glumly. The site of the up sidings is completely obscured.

Rochdale has been famous as a cotton-spinning town, and the Rochdale canal, which runs right by the railway, was prominent as a major broad canal, bolstering that trade. The Co-operative movement was founded in Rochdale although the modern headquarters is in Manchester. Rochdale was also

Fig. 208   Castleton East Junction and Rochdale West signal boxes, October 2014.

Fig. 209   Rochdale signal box, March 2006.

the home of the singer, actor and entertainer Gracie Fields, who was phenomenally successful and was said to be the first artist in Britain to earn £1,000 a week – at a time when a house could be bought for £350.

Rochdale signal box does not look very happy in Fig. 209, five years before its demise. The centre track is for the bay platform located inside the island platform of the two running lines. Just after the curve is the single-track branch to Oldham, which became double track at Shaw and Crompton station and is our next signal box stop on this line. The bay platform was later just used for empty stock or as a turnback siding for a late-running Todmorden service on the way to Bradford across the Pennines.

Fig. 210 shows Rochdale station looking towards Castleton. The L&Y buildings have gone but the station had eight platforms, of which four were bays. The bay platform has only one road now, on the right, and the high-intensity red lights are to guard against a train overrunning the buffers. Many sites like this have train protection and warning system (TPWS) grids, which will apply the brakes if a train approaches too quickly.

Rochdale station appears again in Fig. 211. A Northern Trains class 150 DMU is approaching from Castleton, and the snowplough-type object on the front looks as though it might be needed. The remains of one of the old platforms are on the left.

From Rochdale the line splits and the double track continues to Smithy Bridge, which is where

Fig. 211   Rochdale station and class 150 arriving from Manchester, March 2006.

Fig. 210   Rochdale station and bay platform, March 2006.

we shall pick this journey up on the way to Bradford over the Pennines to Yorkshire. In the meantime the single track branches off for Shaw and Crompton towards Oldham.

Shaw Station

Date Built	1941
LYR Type or Builder	L&Y 2h+
No. of Levers	24
Way of Working	AB
Current Status	Demolished 2010
Listed Y/N	N

Fig. 212   Shaw Station signal box, March 2006.

From the nineteenth century Shaw grew from being little more than a village to a town with forty-eight of the largest cotton mills in Britain.

The last cotton spinning was done in the town in 1989, but six of the forty-eight mills survive in other use. The station was well equipped with stone station buildings and massive goods shed and yard, no doubt to service all the mills.

The box had been in store as part of the LMS war reserve and was called up part way through the war.

In Fig. 212 it looks as though it was built with the blast-proof ground floor as a wartime measure. Note the London Midland Region maroon name plate and one of the last mills in the background.

Shaw station itself is shown in Fig. 213, with the box on the right. The line is going towards Oldham Mumps. Another one of the six mills is on the left. To get an idea of what Shaw Station had been like, see the section on Hebden Bridge in the Manchester to Bradford section.

Fig. 214 shows Shaw station looking the other way, towards Rochdale, and single track. The buffer stops on the left-hand track are just visible beyond the second crossover. The East Lancashire Railway were looking to save Shaw station signal box but a survey found asbestos, which is ruinously expensive to remove. Certain equipment from the box was saved for the ELR, however, and the enamel name plate has been preserved.

Fig. 213   Shaw Station signal box looking towards Oldham Mumps, March 2006.

Fig. 214   Shaw Station looking towards Rochdale, March 2006.

Oldham Mumps (OM)

Date Built	1967
LYR Type or Builder	BR LMR Type 15
No. of Levers	IFS Panel
Way of Working	TCB
Current Status	Demolished 2010
Listed (Y/N)	N

Oldham nestles on the side of the Pennines and was relatively unknown until the nineteenth century. During the Industrial Revolution the town became one of the first industrialized towns and was a massive centre for cotton spinning. At its peak its cotton output exceeded that of France and Germany combined. Cotton spinning ceased in 1998. Two spin-offs from cotton were engineering works to manufacture cotton industry machines, and structural engineering. There was also a coalfield that had up to 150 pits operating at once. Nowadays there is still an electronics presence in the town with Ferranti Technologies, who manufactured analogue navigation systems for ships and aircraft as well as other systems.

Here the Oldham loop is almost complete, and from the farthest distance away at Rochdale we have come back to within a few miles of Manchester.

Oldham Mumps station was the last survivor of the seven stations in Oldham. Trains from Manchester Victoria had to start off at an altitude of 100ft (30m), then climb to 600ft (180m) at Oldham Mumps in about 6 miles (10km). As the station was so close to Manchester, it is, not surprisingly,

track circuit block with colour light signals. Fig. 215 shows the box 'with the builders in', dated 2006. The box is surrounded by the impedimenta of TCB with relay rooms and storage containers.

Oldham Mumps station was typical L&Y with the overall canopy and island platform with bay between the platforms, as shown in Fig. 216. The station building itself was demolished but the canopies were saved by the East Lancashire Railway for their own use.

Fig. 217 shows a class 150 departing for Manchester Victoria past signal OM23.

The fine brickwork of Oldham Mumps station is clearly to be seen in Fig. 218. The bay platform was down the opposite end and had been turned into a garden, although the buffer stops defeated the gardeners and remained to the last.

Fig. 215   Oldham Mumps signal box, June 2006.

Fig. 216   Oldham Mumps station and inset bay platform, June 2006.

Fig. 217   Oldham Mumps station with a class 150 departing for Manchester Victoria, June 2006.

Fig. 218   Oldham Mumps yellow brick station building and L&Y canopies, June 2006.

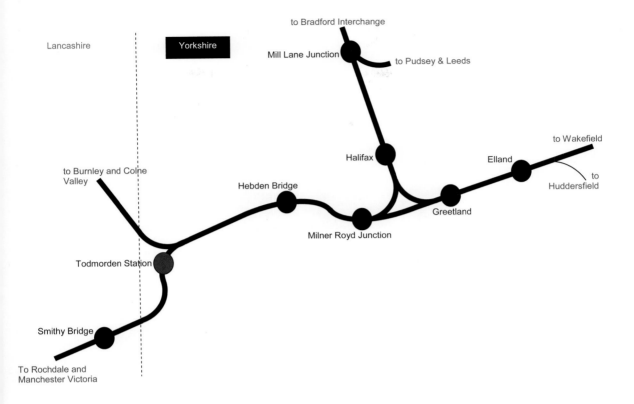

Fig. 219   Manchester–Bradford schematic diagram.

Manchester to Bradford

Fig. 219 is a simplified schematic diagram that shows the journey starting where we left off, near Rochdale, and heading into Yorkshire. The route crosses the Pennines via tunnels, sharp curves and a few viaducts. Although the scenery can rival the Settle–Carlisle in places, the route is much more built up, largely thanks to the railway in the first place. Rochdale was the last of the cotton-spinning towns on the west side of the Pennines and was the centre of the wool processing industry, although other textiles, such as velvet and silk, were also manufactured here. There were fifty-six mills in Bradford alone.

Some of the mills have been regenerated into apartments, restaurants, retail outlets and museums and art galleries. The survey takes in the now demolished boxes of Greetland and Elland, east of Bradford.

Smithy Bridge (SB)

Date Built	1903 (originally 1874)
LYR Type or Builder	L&Y (Yardley)
No. of Levers	IFS Panel
Way of Working	AB, TCB
Current Status	Demolished 2014
Listed (Y/N)	N

Fig. 220   Smithy Bridge signal box, March 2006.

Fig. 221   Rear of Smithy Bridge signal box, March 2006.

Smithy Bridge had a small part to play before the railway age as it was on the packhorse route to Yorkshire. It still has its station but the signal box was demolished when Rochdale West signal box came into being (*see* the section on Castleton East Junction above).

Smithy Bridge signal box started life as Smithy Bridge East in 1874, so there was more than one box here. The bottom half of the box was from that date but the top half was a mere youngster from the twentieth century. Fig. 220 shows a box in good condition with really only the windows and blanked-off end window as testament to the twenty-first century. Inside it was quite different as the box only had an IFS panel instead of a frame, as it was in TCB territory.

The rear of Smithy Bridge signal box in Fig. 221 has the usual lookout window for a box on a crossing. Note the patch in the roof slates where the stove pipe would have appeared from and the flue of the replacement gas heater discolouring the cladding above it. The brick-built, buttress-like structure even suggests there had been a coal fireplace in 1874 Yardley days, but the steps are twenty-first century.

From here the line climbs through the Summit Tunnels, the longest of which is 1 mile and 1,125yd (2.6km) to Todmorden; it is near here, at Hall Royd

Junction, that the junction is to be made triangular to enable trains from Rochdale to reach Burnley and Colne. This change has been promised for 2015. The line continues through a succession of tunnels to reach the first signal box in Yorkshire at Hebden Bridge.

Hebden Bridge (HB)

Date Built	1891
LYR Type or Builder	L&Y
No. of Levers	38
Way of Working	TCB, AB
Current Status	Active
Listed (Y/N)	Y (2013)

Hebden Bridge is a small town in the Calder Valley, which in the nineteenth century gained a reputation for garment manufacture and was dubbed 'Trouser Town' in tribute. The town now has many commuters to the major population centres both sides of it and has become popular with young professionals.

Hebden Bridge signal box (Fig. 222), like the rest of the station, is as close to original L&Y condition as can be found and no doubt this was a factor in its recent listing. The box is almost exactly, externally at least, as it would have been in former days. The windows are even replacement wooden frames

Fig. 222 Hebden Bridge signal box, November 2004.

Fig. 223 Hebden Bridge station looking towards Manchester, November 2004.

rather than the popular uPVC elsewhere. They do not look quite right as they have put on weight thanks to double glazing. However this is a minor point.

Outside the box the way of working is track circuit block to Rochdale West (formerly Smithy Bridge) and absolute block to Milner Royd Junction. There is a trailing crossover and a refuge siding on the up side, which is towards Manchester.

Fig. 223 could have been taken before World War I except for the attire of the passengers. It might be interesting to offer discount tickets to those who turn up in Edwardian dress, reminiscent of the Leeds City Varieties theatre.

Perhaps the most striking feature is the signage followed by the facilities. There really is a booking office, toilets and a delightful café at the time of the survey. Details such as the replica gas lamps and original stone slabs or 'flags' for the platform surface enhance the scene. The platform edging, however, is concrete 3ft by 2ft (0.9m × 0.6m) slabs. The far

platform face has an opening, boarded off, and this is usually the place where the point rodding and signal wires would find their way out from a signal box on the platform, or levers in a station building. No record can be found to confirm this and this would pre-date 1860. The station opened in 1840.

It is something of a transport hub, as buses stop here and there is a large car park where the goods yard was. There had been a massive goods shed here and it had been so busy that a capstan was provided for the rope shunting of wagons. The capstan would be spun using a foot treadle to stop or change direction. A rope would be attached to the W iron of the wagon underframe by a steel hook and the wagon pulled along by wrapping the rope quickly round the capstan. Once the wagon was on the move the big problem was stopping it – the shunter had to apply the wagon brakes with a pole jammed on top of the brake lever, using the underframe as a fulcrum. Capstans could be steam driven.

Fig. 224 Hebden Bridge station and a class 150 waiting to depart to Manchester, November 2004.

Fig. 225   Hebden Bridge signal box full frontal, November 2004.

galvanized steel dustbin seems in period. Perhaps the hi-vis jackets inside the box are another indicator. It is unusual for the small windows beneath the sliding ones to be restored; they are usually just blanked off.

Hebden Bridge is 23 miles and 50 chains (38km) from Manchester Victoria station.

Milner Royd Junction (HB)

Date Built	1874
LYR Type or Builder	Yardley Type 2 (L&Y)
No. of Levers	20
Way of Working	AB
Current Status	Active
Listed (Y/N)	N (Refused)

A class 150 waits to depart for Manchester in Fig. 224, and the red colour light signal refers to the Bradford-bound platform. It is apparent that the line is bi-directionally signalled in a sort of signalling AC/DC. This is quite common, as reverting to single-line working in the past involved lots of people to clip catch points, give hand signals and various other complicated operations where a train was travelling with the signals facing what had become the wrong way. It is obviously cheaper to signal it all twice.

It is just the modern housing behind the signal box that gives the period away in Fig. 225. Even the

Sources date Milner Royd Junction signal box (Fig. 226) variously to 1874 and or 1878. Details can be hazy in the mists of this much time. However, it is definitely early and Yardley and Smith, and they were superseded by the Railway Signalling Company of Liverpool before the L&Y started building their own signal boxes in 1881. It was thought to be a candidate for listing but has been turned down by English Heritage. Access to the box would be a problem, as it is not near a station or road crossing and if the box is not visited and looked after it may fall down in time.

The diagram inside the signal box in Fig. 227 shows the simple double junction track layout. The alternating different-coloured strips punctuated by double red light clusters are track circuits. When a train is standing on a circuit those two lamps light up – there are two in case one fails. When the train leaves the circuit, it is reset and the lights go out. If the train is not in view from the box it is possible to chart its progress through the section by watching the lights illuminate and then extinguish.

The two orange strips either side of the track are a representation of Sowerby Bridge station and before that, on the right, the 657yd (601m) Sowerby Bridge tunnel. In the same direction but not shown on the diagram, as it is not in this box's section, is Hebden

Fig. 226   Milner Royd Junction signal box, December 2007.

Bridge and beyond. The tracks below the main running lines are the junction to Bradford, with the 214yd (196m) Bank House tunnel in the distance. The running lines continue to the left to Mirfield and Wakefield. At the time of the survey, the next box was Greetland in the Wakefield direction.

Moving down below the diagram, the blue-painted shelf is known as the block shelf as it primarily supports the absolute block instruments. At the far end of the block shelf are two L&Y block instruments, which are used to establish and indicate the status of the track: Blocked or normal, Line Clear or Train on Line. There is another modernized block instrument for communication with Greetland.

The single-strike block bells with what looks like an outsize bicycle bell on top of them are used to signal to each box what the line status is and what trains are offered and accepted to run. A set of bell codes is used for this purpose.

The block instruments are interlocked with the track circuits in such a way that it is not possible to accept a train into the section if the points and signals are not set up for the accepted route or there is a train already in the section.

Single strike means the bell is pressed once and it rings in the other signal box once. The bells usually have different-sized or -shaped bells on them so that a signaller can determine which bell has rung by its tone. The two bells towards the right-hand end have had a modification in the shape of the signaller's duster. This feature, as well as altering the ring, can quieten the bell down a bit too. Other unofficial devices for altering the tone or quietening are clothes pegs or wads of paper.

This box is doing exactly what it was designed to do when it was first built but automation has reduced the amount of equipment needed to do it, so although it was built with twenty levers (Fig. 228), not all those levers are now needed. The white-painted levers are those no longer in use, and the ones that are in use are all cut down as they only operate switches to change power-operated signals and points. The blue facing-point lock levers are retained to maintain the locking, as power-operated points do not normally need facing-point lock

Fig. 227   Milner Royd Junction signal box interior and diagram, December 2007.

Fig. 228   Milner Royd Junction signal box interior and lever frame, December 2007.

levers. The red annular discs hanging from the block shelf are lever collars, which are applied over the lever handle as a physical reminder that a lever is not to be pulled. They were originally invented to act as an aide-memoire to a signaller who had a train standing at a signal. Track circuiting has done away with this requirement but these are still needed if a signal is being worked on.

The black rectangular object on the block shelf is signal status indicators. They light up with the aspect currently being shown by the signal.

Fig. 229 *Milner Royd Junction signal box desk and register, December 2007.*

Fig. 230 *Milner Royd Junction exterior steps and side view, December 2007.*

Signallers have to check that a signal selection made is answered by the equipment in the case of signals that are not visible from the box. There is another type of signal status indicator that is adapted from semaphore signal position indicators. The circular device with the yellow insert is a distant signal status indicator, but rather than show the colour, it shows whether the signal is on – proceed with caution – or off – proceed. There is another position of 'wrong', which will be displayed if the power to the signal position equipment has failed. There are other indicators to tell if the power supply to the signal head has failed. These supplies

are nearly always backed up with an uninterruptible power supply or UPS. There are two more circular devices on the block shelf with a black knob in the middle. These are 'Welwyn Releases', which enable the locking of the block instruments and track circuits to be released after a set time interval, should the signaller wish to override the interlock in the case of a track circuit relay or other failure.

Milner Royd Junction is extraordinarily compact, as Fig. 229 amply illustrates. The register on the desk at the far wall, where every bell code is recorded, is the nineteenth-century version of the tachygraph or flight data recorder. In complete contrast, the white cabinet in the corner is a 19in rack module used to mount trays that contain industrial versions of personal computers and communications kit. The TRUST computer system produces a running commentary on where the trains are, which direction they are travelling in and punctuality details. The signaller's chair and Sunday paper complete the working scene.

Although Milner Royd Junction signal box is a heritage location, modern methods are needed to protect the box, with grilles on the windows and a steel gate in front of the door, as shown in Fig. 230. Note the bags of salt for the signal box steps in icy conditions.

Milner Royd Junction is 29 miles and 20 chains (47km) from Manchester Victoria station.

Halifax (H)

Date Built	1884
LYR Type or Builder	Robert Stephenson and Co. (L&Y)
No. of Levers	IFS Panel
Way of Working	AB
Current Status	Active
Listed (Y/N)	N

Halifax came to prominence with the upsurge in the woollen trade in the late eighteenth century. There was an early wool traders' market at Piece Hall. The town also developed woollen carpet manufacture with Crossley carpets, while Mackintosh's confectionery and chocolate products are known the world over. Mackintosh's were taken over by Rowntree's of York, who then succumbed to Nestlé in the 1980s. The Halifax Bank, meanwhile, is the largest provider of mortgages in the United Kingdom.

The railway facilities at Halifax were pivotal to the town's success, and some evidence remains of the large station although the goods shed and yards have gone. There were two signal boxes at the station and Halifax so called was once Halifax East.

Halifax signal box, in Fig. 231, retains the distinctive Robert Stephenson and Company (RSCo) scalloped barge boards at the ends of the roof. The box had a seventy-lever frame for the semaphore signalling installation. The original size of the station can be gauged by the disused platform edge with the buddleia growing out of it. Behind the box were more platforms, originally 5 and 6, from the Queensbury route that linked Halifax, Keighley and Bradford by the Great Northern Railway, later LNER. This line closed in 1958 as it was a duplication to some extent of Midland Railway lines in the area.

Inside the box the IFS panel and block instrument were made up at York as, after nationalization, Halifax became part of the North Eastern Region of British Railways despite its LMS/L&Y origins.

Fig. 232 shows the view of Halifax station looking south towards Milner Royd Junction and Greetland. The station has been heavily modernized but some of the original features remain inside. The Queensbury route remains can be seen on the far right and the box is on the disused island platform.

Finally at Halifax, the true shape of the original station is revealed in the box placement, looking north (Fig. 233). The box stood in a Y of lines with the aforementioned Queensbury route coming in from the left.

The trailing crossover precedes the Beacon Hill tunnel, which is 1,105yd (1,010m) long.

At the other end of the station there are two more crossovers, facing and trailing, and these are to grant access to what is termed a reversing siding but is now used to accommodate empty coaching stock

Fig. 231   Halifax signal box, August 2008.

Fig. 232   Halifax station with disused platforms on the right, August 2008.

Fig. 233   Halifax signal box showing its angled position, August 2008.

Fig. 234   Mill Lane Junction signal box, August 2007.

Fig. 235   Mill Lane Junction signal box and end view, August 2007.

and as a turnback facility for trains from Bradford and New Pudsey. The brick structure on the end of the box is the relay room for the track circuits and associated equipment.

Mill Lane Junction (ML)

Date Built	1884
LYR Type or Builder	Robert Stephenson and Co. (L&Y)
No. of Levers	IFS Panel
Way of Working	AB, TCB
Current Status	Active
Listed (Y/N)	N

We move on to Bradford now and a city that experienced phenomenal growth in the nineteenth century, when it was known as 'the wool capital of the world'. One notable industrialist, Titus Salt, moved a little way out of Bradford to found the village of Saltaire, now a UNESCO world heritage site. In recent years the city has become home to the National Media Museum and is also the headquarters of the William Morrison supermarket chain.

The original ten-platform Bradford Exchange station was a cathedral to railways and a joint venture between the Lancashire and Yorkshire and Great Northern Railways, although there was no physical connection unless via Mill Lane Junction. Expresses to King's Cross left on the Great Northern route through Wakefield Westgate and Doncaster from the east side of the station.

It was demolished and rebuilt on a different site, merged with the bus station and renamed Bradford Interchange with four platforms and mostly local services.

Mill Lane Junction (Fig. 234) controls the route into Bradford Interchange and the branch to New Pudsey and Leeds, which has a Great Northern Railway origin. The line out to New Pudsey passes Hammerton Street, which was a Great Northern locomotive depot that housed the myriad tank engines needed to service the intensive suburban services. The depot was bombed during World War II and lost its distinctive roof over the running roads. It was subsequently converted into a DMU depot and later on closed altogether.

Mill Lane Junction signal box has been heavily modernized in Fig. 235, with tilt-up windows and curiously GWR-like handrails across some of the windows. It fringes to York power box to the east towards Leeds, and at the time of the survey,

Fig. 236   Greetland signal box, August 2007.

Fig. 237   Greetland signal box rear view, August 2007.

Greetland, back on the former L&Y main line, to Wakefield. Since the closure of Greetland it now interfaces to Healey Mills near Mirfield.

Greetland

Date Built	1941
LYR Type or Builder	LMS Type 13
No. of Levers	55
Way of Working	AB
Current Status	Demolished 2009
Listed (Y/N)	N

Greetland signal box was another of the LMS ARP-style boxes brought into use during World War II. After many years of disuse the box was brought back into operation in 2000. The eastern side of the triangle was closed off to traffic and the box's sole purpose was to control this function. However, in 2000 a service from Halifax to Huddersfield was reinstated and this needed the box back in service.

Fig. 237 shows Greetland signal box from the rear and side. The box was on the platform of Greetland station, which closed in 1962. The site behind the box was retained for some years, until 1998 at least,

for Wayahead Fuels (who are no longer trading). Greetland was not far away from Low Moor L&Y locomotive depot, which was home to ex-LMS and ex-LNER engines after it became part of the North Eastern Region. Low Moor was famous for keeping its locomotives in spick and span condition, which was no mean feat under the conditions. Low Moor was one of the last steam sheds to close in the former West Riding of Yorkshire.

Greetland signal box was 30 miles and 77 chains (49.8km) from Manchester Victoria station.

Elland

Date Built	1958
LYR Type or Builder	BR NER Type 17
No. of Levers	60
Way of Working	AB, TCB
Current Status	Demolished 2009
Listed (Y/N)	N

Elland signal box architecture (Fig. 238) can be described as the suburban post-war style of the North Eastern Region. It too lay closed for some years after the junction from the Wakefield line to Halifax was unused. It reopened in 2000 but was

Fig. 238   Elland signal box, August 2007.

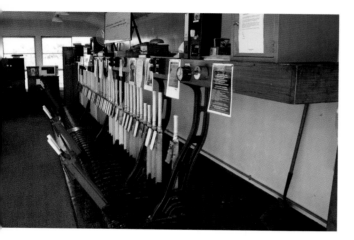

Fig. 239   Elland signal box interior and lever frame, August 2007.

Fig. 240   Elland signal box interior and block shelf, August 2007.

also demolished in 2009 when Healey Mills, near Mirfield, took over its duties.

Healey Mills was one of the massive marshalling yards introduced by British Railways in the 1960s at just the time when road transport was in the ascendant for freight, and traditional loose-coupled freight trains that had to be sorted and marshalled every so often were on their way out. The yard has been disused for years but Healey Mills box remains forlornly in the middle of it all.

Elland signal box architecture may have been prosaic but the lever frame, whilst not a symphony in cast iron, is at least a concerto. The lever frame in Fig. 239 is a Mackenzie and Holland product, whose company merged with others in 1901.

An extremely simple layout from the diagram is shown, with just plain double track. The block bell on the left is to communicate with Healey Mills in an emergency and there is no absolute block instrument here for that box, as it is TCB. Further along the block shelf is a British Railways domino-style absolute block instrument to communicate with Greetland. It has its block bell integral with the instrument. It looks as though there are six signal levers in use and the rest are disused.

Fig. 240 shows the signal box block shelf in detail, or some of it at least. The domino BR block instrument was so called because it was made up out of black and white modules that stack one on another.

The indicators are divided into two, down and up, with up on top. The signaller at Elland selects either Line Clear and then Train on Line when a train is sent in Elland's direction on the down line towards Wakefield. This is to advise the sending box of the line's status, and the position is reflected by indicator in both boxes.

Similarly, when Elland is sending Greetland a train on the up line towards Manchester, the Greetland signaller has to select Line Clear first on the Greetland instrument, and this is reflected on the top indicator at Elland.

All this is interlocked with signals and track circuits so that the signaller, before giving Line Clear at the receiving box, must pull off the signals relevant to the move and there must be no train in the section, as detected by the track circuit, before the Line Clear selection will actually work.

This is a Welwyn Control, named after an accident in 1935 on the LNER where a signaller accepted a train into a section that was already occupied by a train standing at the station.

The Welwyn Release, which is the grey cylindrical device with the handle screwed to the block shelf, will override the control in exceptional conditions.

The cylindrical device below the domino is some kind of interlock with the next box. Very often the next box will have to release a switch to enable a function to take place at the original box. This is a kind of inter-box interlock.

The indicators to the left are showing the colour light signals. The Bardic lamp next to the domino on the block shelf is to signal to trains with different-coloured lights in the event of a total power failure. The signaller also has flags in three colours for the same purpose. The locked cabinet on the right may contain detonators, which are used in fog or falling

snow as a stop signal to a train when placed on the rails.

Elland signal box was 31 miles and 66 chains (51.2km) from Manchester Victoria station, so a short section from Greetland.

From here the line continues east past a junction with a single line to Huddersfield after which is Mirfield station, where there was an L&Y locomotive depot that was a fairly ordinary place until Healey Mills opened in the early 1960s. Thenceforth it was inundated with steam locos from far and wide.

Preston to Blackpool North

This line has been given the deadline of 2016 for all mechanical signalling to be removed.

The line starts off from Preston, which is a track circuit block area across the rich farmland of the Fylde plain to Kirkham, where the line originally split into three to approach Blackpool in some sort of railway pincer movement. The northern and southern approaches survive, and to the

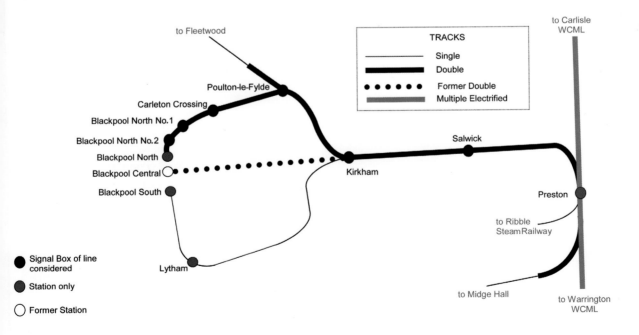

Fig. 241 Preston–Blackpool North schematic diagram.

north there is Poulton-le-Fylde with semaphores, and then a fairly sharp curve into Blackpool North No. 2, which is a veritable forest of signals. Seaside resorts, Southport excepted, seem to hang onto their semaphores longer. Examples of this around the country in recent years are or were Skegness, Great Yarmouth, Scarborough, Bridlington, Rhyl, Prestatyn, Llandudno, Holyhead, Bognor Regis and Littlehampton at the survey dates.

There were four L&Y signal boxes in Preston, of which none has survived but the first on the Blackpool line, which is Salwick.

Salwick (SK)

Date Built	1889
LYR Type or Builder	Robert Stephenson and Co. (L&Y)
No. of Levers	33
Way of Working	TCB
Current Status	Active
Listed (Y/N)	N

Salwick was host to a down goods loop (towards Blackpool) and some sidings on the down side connected with British Nuclear Fuels. They appear to have been disused for some years. The Springfields Plant was converted from a 1940 munitions factory to a plant that manufactured fuel rods for nuclear power stations; it has a role to play for some years yet.

Salwick signal box, shown in Fig. 242, is simply a functional signal box with no attempt to maintain its original appearance or even in sympathy with it. Gone are the roof slates, walkway and ladders, although one roof finial has survived.

It has the London Midland Region enamelled name plate, which tells us this was Salwick No. 2 at some point.

Salwick box is 5 miles 3 chains (8.1km) from Preston station.

Kirkham (KM)

Date Built	1903
LYR Type or Builder	L&Y+
No. of Levers	76
Way of Working	TCB, AB
Current Status	Active
Listed (Y/N)	N

Kirkham was originally Kirkham North Junction with 105 levers. The L&Y built another line to Blackpool to Central station. That made three, the same as the number of piers the town has. To accommodate the Wakes Week traffic, when whole towns in Lancashire would shut down for a week for their holiday, Central station and the massive junction at Kirkham were created.

Fig. 242   Salwick signal box, February 2006.

Fig. 243   Kirkham signal box, August 2005.

Fig. 244   Kirkham signal box and junctions, August 2005.

Fig. 245   Kirkham station environs, August 2005.

To illustrate how busy Kirkham was, Blackpool Central station was the world's busiest station in 1911, with fourteen platforms and numerous storage sidings for visiting trains, and it all passed through Kirkham. In addition, there was traffic to Blackpool North, Fleetwood and Blackpool South.

In Fig. 243 you can clearly see where the 'North Junction' part of the name board was. Apart from the first-floor windows and doors the box has an original look to it. Even though we are in a TCB area, note how many point rods emerge from the box.

The lines past Kirkham signal box go briefly into quadruple-track mode, where they are described in Fig. 244 as up fast, down fast, up and down slow, and down slow, reading from the box right to left. The fifth line on the far left is to Lytham and Blackpool South. Kirkham and Wesham station lies between the two slow lines and the other tracks are, in effect, loops to enable excursion trains to bypass stopping trains at the station. The loops are just over a mile long. The tracks had been quadruple track as far as Preston in busier times.

There are also engineer's sidings, which run off a spur that was once the down line to Lytham before that line was made single track. Trains to Blackpool South are worked on the one train working (OTW) principle, where there is no staff or token but because the line is completely track circuited it can automatically prevent another train from entering the branch as it knows if one is already on there. There are special arrangements where this interlock can be overridden if a train has broken down in the section and has to be rescued by another train.

After the Blackpool South junction there is a siding running off the down slow line, which leads to Kirkham tip siding, which is a couple of sidings and a loop to enable trains with spent or used ballast to tip their loads. This has been largely disused since the 1980s.

Just after Kirkham station, the goods yard was on the left in Fig. 245 with the goods shed still there in other use. A train is signalled for Blackpool South.

Kirkham signal box is 8 miles 42 chains (13.7km) from Preston station. Note how many tracks there would have been from the overbridge spans. Only one of the three spans now has tracks under it.

Poulton-le-Fylde No. 3 (PT)

Date Built	1896
LYR Type or Builder	L&Y+
No. of Levers	72
Way of Working	AB
Current Status	Active
Listed (Y/N)	N

Poulton-le-Fylde's origins go back to Roman times and beyond. It developed as a port on the River Wyre and became the market hub of the area until

Fig. 246   Poulton-le-Fylde signal box, February 2006.

Fig. 247   Poulton-le-Fylde signal box and Fleetwood line detail, February 2006.

Fig. 248   Poulton-le-Fylde station, with a train expected for Blackpool North, February 2006.

overshadowed by Blackpool and Fleetwood in the nineteenth century. It is now a pleasant market town.

The fact that Poulton signal box was Poulton No. 3 gives us an insight into the levels of railway traffic that once were seen here. The branch line to Fleetwood is just about still there as a freight-only line. Fleetwood had been a deep-sea fishing port that generated massive traffic as well as a quieter alternative to Blackpool as a seaside resort. Fleetwood, Grimsby and Hull were the largest fishing ports in Britain.

The passenger station closed in 1966, no doubt hastened by the fact that the Blackpool seafront tram system's northern terminus is Fleetwood. Fleetwood was also developed as a cargo and ferry port but both of these activities have now ceased. Including Poulton No. 5, there were nine absolute block signal boxes on the Fleetwood branch.

Fig. 246 sees Poulton signal box right at the junction of the Blackpool and Fleetwood lines, still proclaiming its origins in the name plate. The overgrown line to Fleetwood appears to be double track but reduces to single within half a mile. The down track to Fleetwood on the left has a catch point and the up line on the right a trap point. The box has been uPVC'd to the nth degree on the first floor but still retains a slate roof. Note the point rodding coming out of the box from the front and rear.

Fig. 247 shows more detail of the Fleetwood freight-only line and trailing crossover in what is actually a loop. The double-decker ground discs are for reversing over the crossover: the lower is for the crossover itself and the upper for the following point at either end of the loop. They all appear to be track circuited, a legacy from the passenger-carrying days, no doubt. The back lights on the far discs show up well and would be covered up by a small white arm, when selected off, to indicate to the signaller they have moved. The signal box wooden steps are just visible.

Fig. 248 shows the down platform towards Blackpool, with a Blackpool North train expected at Poulton-le-Fylde station. The branch to Fleetwood on the right is on a sharp curve and therefore signalled at a lower speed from the signal post or doll height. The station building is a fine example in what looks like Ruabon red brick. The down refuge siding is on the left. The layout is classic L&Y with an island platform and some station buildings up on the road above. The Great Central Railway used a similar approach – Loughborough station is a good example.

Poulton le Fylde station is 14 miles 31 chains (23.2km) from Preston station.

Carleton Crossing (CN)

Fig. 249   Carleton Crossing signal box, May 2007.

Date Built	1924
LYR Type or Builder	LNWR 5+
No. of Levers	12
Way of Working	AB
Current Status	Active
Listed (Y/N)	N

An interloper in the L&Y midst, this London and North Western Box (Fig. 249) was built by the LMS. Before they got their act together and designed their own, they used other companies' designs, although the box does have an L&Y frame. The frame has been reduced over the years, no doubt when the lifting barriers were introduced in 1977 and the gates were done away with. Of the twelve levers only four remain operational. There are two home and two distant signals and the reduced lever size on signal 6 in the up Poulton direction suggests this is a colour light. There are two BR 'domino' block instruments for the absolute block working with Poulton and Blackpool. Note that there is a period electric light hanging from the wrought iron bracket and double bars all around the windows.

Fig. 250 looks back from Carleton Crossing box towards Poulton box; the two are exactly one mile apart. In the distance is Poulton's up distant signal. This is quite a short absolute block section and is typical of densely used lines where trains will follow one another rapidly. The home signal belonging to Carleton Crossing has a sighting board on it but it has been configured so it does not obscure the back light and its cover, which face the box. You can see the white curved back light cover that swings up when the signal is pulled off and

Fig. 250   Carleton Crossing with Preston home signal and Blackpool distant, May 2007.

Fig. 251   Carleton Crossing signal box, rear view, May 2007.

Fig. 252   Blackpool North No. 1 signal box, August 2005.

covers the light to indicate to the signaller that the signal has answered the lever.

Fig. 251 shows the rear of Carleton Crossing box. The double bars continue round to the crossing lookout windows, and there's a finial present even on the porch. The old lamp hut next door is in the same livery as the box but not faring quite so well.

Blackpool North No. 1 (BN1)

Date Built	1959
LYR Type or Builder	BR London Midland Region 15+
No. of Levers	65
Way of Working	AB
Current Status	Demolished 2011
Listed (Y/N)	N

As well as being an absolute block post, Blackpool North No. 1 controlled the north end of fifteen carriage sidings and the main line exit signals from the station.

The box itself appears to be the very epitome of modernity (Fig. 252) but within were L&Y absolute block instruments. The box was provided with a switch that would enable all its functions to be bypassed and communications then would be between Carleton Crossing and Blackpool North No. 2. This means that all running line signals have to be off or signal arm up.

This facility is invoked whenever the box is not required to have a signaller present. Some boxes are not open evenings and weekends and must therefore have a switch.

Being able to switch the box out, coupled with the reduction in loco-hauled trains, must make it easier to close the box. Bank holiday excursion trains would leave their parent station early in the morning, pick up en route and arrive usually before lunchtime. The trains would then wait all day in the carriage sidings before returning in the evening. This needed the facilities at Blackpool North No. 1 but the current traffic pattern is to run a more frequent service of DMU-type trains that are not at the station for any appreciable time. The line is to be electrified by 2017.

The layout, at the time of the survey, consists of a pair of up and down running lines and a track parallel to those lines called the through siding, which leaves the down main not far from the box and rejoins the down main opposite No. 2 box, a distance of 3/8 mile (600m). On the opposite side to the

Fig. 253   Blackpool North No. 1 signal box and carriage sidings, August 2005.

box are the twelve carriage sidings, which are actually all loops. Three of the twelve look as though they have carriage-washing facilities.

Beyond the loops is a locomotive loop followed by three sidings, which are at the opposite end of the layout to the box. One of these sidings is a diesel refuelling point.

The through siding is not track circuited and would only be used for shunting or empty stock trains. The exit to all sidings towards the station end is controlled by the No. 2 box.

The double-decker ground disc in front of the box in Fig. 253 is the crossover to the through siding, and the semaphore signal is giving the all clear to a departure towards Preston on the up main. The remnants of yard lamps can be seen, with what looks like signal ladders attached. Back down the yard towards No. 2 box the lamps are in place and modern.

Blackpool North No. 1 signal box was 17 miles exactly (27.3km) from Preston station.

Blackpool North No. 2 (BN2)

Date Built	1896
LYR Type or Builder	L&Y+
No. of Levers	72
Way of Working	AB
Current Status	Active
Listed (Y/N)	N

Originally the box was built with a 120-lever frame and there was a Blackpool North No. 3 box on the scene.

The box is looking a bit careworn in Fig. 254 but we are all indebted to the seagull that is making up for the loss of the finial at the far end. On the front of the box was a maroon London Midland Region 1950s/60s sign that proclaimed Blackpool North station to be this way. One of these types of sign was

still in existence at Liverpool Edge Hill signal box in 2013.

After Blackpool North No. 1 was taken out of service, No. 2 had an IFS panel installed to take over the remaining functionality from the closed box.

In Fig. 255 we can just see all eight platforms at Blackpool North and their starter signals. The six platforms 3 to 8, with 8 on the left, have a bracket signal for each pair of platforms. Platforms 2 and 1 have their starters on single posts, reading from the left. Platform 2 starter also has Blackpool North No. 1's distant on the same post, and a subsidiary arm with route indicator for a siding or loop move. Platform 1's starter, over by Mecca Bingo, was changed later to include the distant signal as well.

Fig. 254   Blackpool North No. 2 signal box, October 2014.

Fig. 255   Blackpool North station starter signals, August 2005.

The six platforms and their bracket signals feed out to other signals that have distants on them as well for the up main line.

From the Mecca Bingo car park in Fig. 256 the signal nearest the concrete fence on the far right is the platform 1 starter, now with a distant arm as well. Note that there is a subsidiary siding signal with 'stencil box' route indicator.

The other two signals route platforms 3 to 8 onto the up main line but they too have the smaller siding arms and stencil boxes. The seagull has abandoned the architectural post to talk to a friend.

Fig. 257 shows the immediate environs of a train leaving Blackpool North on the up main line. Just behind the fence, nearest to the camera, is the through siding loop, then the two running lines, and beyond that the carriage sidings. Just to the left of the Network Rail van is the start of the three locomotive sidings, and beyond the brick buildings is the diesel refuelling point.

Fig. 256   Blackpool North No. 2 signal box station departure signals, October 2014.

Fig. 257 Blackpool North No. 2 carriage sidings and washery, October 2014.

On the down side but not on the running lines, Fig. 258 shows the siding exit signal just to the left of the yard depicted in Fig. 257. The stencil boxes describe where the train will actually go to rather than just give permission to leave the carriage loops.

Further on to the station approach, Fig. 259 shows the down main signal on the left supported by scaffolding; it not only has a theatre-style route indicator for which of the eight platforms to use but also has the red-and-white striped armed signal below it. This is a 'calling on' arm and is used to bring a train into a platform that may already be occupied by another train or locomotive. The way of working is usually to bring the train to a complete stand at the home signal, then pull the calling on arm off, which will also be described on the route indicator. The message here is to proceed with the utmost caution. Even a very low speed collision can result in a fatal event.

There is a further siding signal for the two short sidings that end in buffer stops to the right; these are not track circuited and suitable for a locomotive or perhaps an empty, short DMU. There are three trains in the station at this point in the autumn.

Blackpool Tower is having work done.

Back to platform 1 starter by the fence in the Mecca Bingo car park, Fig. 260 shows that directly behind it is the through siding exit signal and a further exit signal from the carriage loops.

Many of these signals would have appeared on gantries in the past and it must be cheaper and easier to maintain the present layout. Gantries can be difficult to read and this was thought to be partly the cause of the Ladbroke Grove accident in 1999, where thirty-one people died and

Fig. 258 Blackpool North No. 2 carriage sidings exit signal with stencil boxes, October 2014.

Fig. 259   Blackpool North No. 2 arrival signals and station throat, October 2014.

hundreds were injured. Many preserved lines have them, however, and the North Yorkshire Moors Railway have recently restored Falsgrave gantry from Scarborough to working condition; that said, most preserved lines have a maximum speed limit of 25mph (40km/h) under a Light Railway Order.

Blackpool North station is 17 miles 49 chains (28.3km) from Preston station.

North and East Lancashire

The situation in north and east Lancashire is a very patchy one, with little absolute block working and only a few working signal boxes or level crossing frames.

Much of the railway runs through attractive Pennine scenery or the River Ribble valley, which is where this journey begins.

Fig. 260   Blackpool North No. 2 subsidiary and main signals, October 2014.

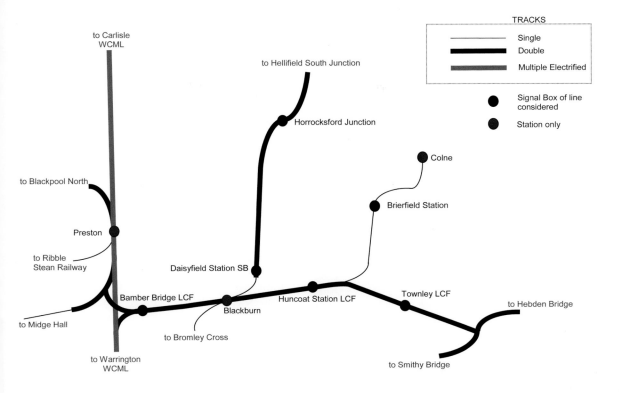

Fig. 261   North and East Lancashire schematic diagram.

The area from Carnforth to Stockport was the last bastion of main line steam working in Britain and some of the places near to the boxes described will be remembered by many as steam's last redoubt in main line service.

East Lancashire

Bamber Bridge Level Crossing Frame

Date Built	1906
LYR Type or Builder	L&Y+
No. of Levers	IFS Panel
Way of Working	Gate
Current Status	Active
Listed (Y/N)	N

As with much of north Lancashire, Bamber Bridge owed its early development to the textile industry and carried on with that for many years despite

distinctly mixed fortunes. The railways had developed significantly in the area, and Lostock Hall near Preston was a significant L&Y loco depot that lasted until 4 August 1968; this was the depot from where all the special trains on the last day of steam working were serviced.

Fig. 262 shows a box with a most unusual construction and seemingly purpose-built for the crossing, with a watchtower-type view of the crossing and approach roads. The box supervises two more crossings to the east by CCTV. There was a trailing crossover and engineer's and private owner sidings nearby but they appear disused. The line is known as the East Lancashire Line.

The reason the box occupies a smaller footprint that the operating room floor is apparent in Fig. 263. The railway line bisects the town and every train more or less brings life to a halt.

Bamber Bridge box is 2 miles 29 chains (3.8km) from the Preston junction, known as Farrington Curve.

Huncoat Level Crossing Frame

Date Built	1902
LYR Type or Builder	L&Y+
No. of Levers	8
Way of Working	Gate
Current Status	Demolished 2013
Listed (Y/N)	N

Huncoat signal box is near Accrington, which was a considerable junction and loco depot that succumbed in 1960 to become a DMU depot. However, Rose Grove on the Blackburn side of the box was one of the last surviving steam sheds in 1968. Textiles and collieries provided most of the freight traffic.

It was announced in January 2013 that the remaining five boxes on this line and their branches, including this one, would close. The line sees seventy-three trains per day and the line speed is 70mph.

The box had originally opened to service a nearby colliery. Note the double height locking frame room with double windows in Fig. 264, some bricked up.

Fig. 262   Bamber Bridge signal box, August 2006.

Fig. 263   Bamber Bridge signal box and crossing, August 2006.

The box had to go because the automatic crossing that replaced it needed the site the box was on for the sensors and equipment for the new crossing. This change had enabled the station to be operated on a mandatory stop rather than a request stop basis.

The crossing type that replaced Huncoat relies on obstacle detection technology using radar to control signals.

Fig. 264   Huncoat level crossing frame signal box, May 2007.

Towneley LCF

Date Built	1878
LYR Type or Builder	Saxby & Farmer Type 9 (L&Y)
No. of Levers	IFS Panel
Way of Working	Gate
Current Status	Closed 2013
Listed (Y/N)	N

Nearby Burnley was another textile town with coal mining thrown in. Bob Lord tried to arrest the post-war decline in textiles in the town and was successful for a time. He also supported Burnley football club and they too prospered for a while.

Towneley level crossing frame (Fig. 265) was another of the gate boxes that was due for demolition and is remarkably similar to Parbold, on the Southport–Wigan line. Parbold is listed so it seems unlikely there would be a reprieve for this box. Towneley is also near Gannow Junction for the Colne branch and Copy Pit, which was celebrated in steam days as venue for photographers. Steam was working against the collar in that area and once again the freight was coal.

The box originally had a twenty-eight-lever frame and was designated Towneley West. The nearby colliery closed in 1951, together with its box, and the box was then renamed Towneley station. There are three stations in Burnley so Towneley station did not survive.

It finally became Towneley LCF when all control of signals was removed to Preston power box in 1973. It is remarkable that structures like this lasted so long.

Fig. 266   Towneley level crossing frame signal box, rear view, May 2007.

Fig. 265   Towneley level crossing frame signal box, May 2007.

Fig. 267   Daisyfield signal box, August 2006.

Fig. 268   Horrocksford Junction signal box, August 2006.

Towneley LCF was 22 miles and 46 chains (36.3km) from Farrington Curve near Preston.

The East Lancashire Line continues for another 8 miles (13km) until it reaches the Rochdale–Hebden Bridge line at Hall Royd Junction.

North Lancashire

This line connects the town of Blackburn and the East Lancashire Line to Hellifield and the Settle–Carlisle Line.

Blackburn was long associated with the textile industry and steel stockholding.

Daisyfield Station (DS)

Date Built	1873
LYR Type or Builder	Saxby & Farmer Type 6 (L&Y)
No. of Levers	16
Way of Working	TCB, AB
Current Status	Active
Listed (Y/N)	Y (2013)

One of the earliest boxes on Network Rail and recently recognized for listing by English Heritage, Daisyfield Station signal box, in Fig. 267, contents itself with just the name Daisyfield, presumably – as the station closed in 1958 – to avoid hopeful passengers turning up. It is still possible to see the old platforms from a passing train. The junction is about half a mile east from Blackburn station and is single track but there are facing and trailing crossovers to enable trains to access the branch.

At the box there are also manually operated level crossing gates. Note the converted oil lamp with a padlock on top of one of the gates.

The box works TCB to Preston power box and AB to Horrocksford Junction up the line towards Hellifield. The line to Horrocksford Junction has intermediate block sections (IBS) in both directions. The freight traffic off the Settle–Carlisle must be considerable for this requirement. As the exit from the branch is onto Preston's patch, the signals are 'slotted' or interlocked so that Preston must authorize any traffic coming off the branch with Daisyfield.

Horrocksford Junction (H)

Date Built	1873
LYR Type or Builder	Saxby & Farmer Type 6 (L&Y)
No. of Levers	8
Way of Working	AB
Current Status	Active
Listed (Y/N)	N (Refused 2013)

With two Saxby & Farmer Type 6 boxes on the same line, English Heritage were probably only going to list one, and that was Daisyfield.

Fig. 269   Horrocksford Junction home signal, August 2006.

Fig. 270   Brierfield Station signal box, May 2007.

The box (Fig. 268) is located near Clitheroe railway station. Oddly the period name plate is located on the relay room next door, in the far right of the picture. The present passenger service extends only as far as Clitheroe and is turned back over the crossover here.

The junction in the name plate is for Ribblesdale Cement Works, and this is accessed from both running lines by a crossover, part of which is a single slip. For an illustration of a single slip and its way of working, *see* Fig. 5 and the piece about Lowdham in Nottinghamshire in Chapter 2.

The cement works line closed in the early 1990s but reopened in 2008.

There is a mixture of colour light and semaphores here, but signal number 2 at Horrocksford Junction is illustrated in Fig. 269. With the extra platform there has been another signal on the same post in the past, and the yellow signal status position indicator can be seen below the arm. There is a telephone on a separate small post in front of

the signal post and it has a black-and-white striped pattern on it. The meaning of this is that any driver whose train is brought to a stand at the signal must call the box to report in, according to rule 55. There is no track circuit lozenge on the post so this must be the reason why a call is mandatory.

Colne

This is a rather isolated town at the end of the branch line from Burnley that witnessed wholesale decline in the textile industry in common with many other places in Lancashire, but now a vibrant retail park has taken the place of one of the mills. The sylvan and hilly scenery round about has inspired a mini house-building boom and the M65 motorway is a vital link. There is also a presence from Rolls Royce, who manufacture precision turbine blades for their aero engines at Barnoldswick nearby.

Brierfield Station

Date Built	1876
LYR Type or Builder	Saxby & Farmer Type 8 (L&Y)
No. of Levers	IFS Panel
Way of Working	TCB, OTW
Current Status	Closed Removed
Listed (Y/N)	N

Brierfield Station is another old-timer in the signal box world but one that may see a future. In Fig. 270 the box literally stands in the way of progress as the obstruction-detection technology using radar requires a clear line of sight to work and the box would have been in the way. The LMR maroon name plate is a piece of heritage Railwayana.

A campaign was launched on Facebook by local people to save the box, and as a result it has been dismantled and stored for future re-erection.

Beyond Brierfield Station the box worked one train working to Colne.

Brierfield Station is 24 miles and 20 chains (39km) from Farrington Curve near Preston.

West Yorkshire

We have been here before but what concerns us now are the remnants of signal boxes that are left once the identifiable routes have been covered on the Lancashire and Yorkshire Railway.

From a total of around 1,000 coal mines before World War I, we have been reduced to just one pit where deep-mined coal is produced in the country, at Hatfield near Doncaster. There is some opencast coal mining going on where the tops of existing coal seams have been uncovered and the coal is quarried rather than mined. It has become much cheaper to import coal from overseas – the flood of cheap American coal available due to shale gas and oil taking coal's place in the US for power generation only adds to the uneconomic nature of deep mining in Britain.

These remaining boxes in West Yorkshire are surrounded by coal-fired power stations that were built close to the coalfields that supplied them. Some are changing their power profile from coal to coal/biomass where biomass is basically wood pellets imported from the US. Coal traffic is still

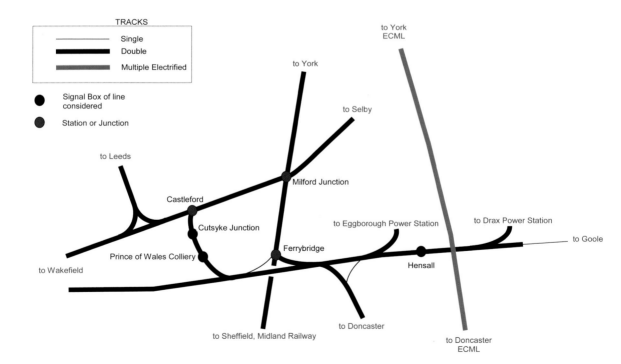

Fig. 271   West Yorkshire schematic diagram.

heavy but mainly from Immingham docks, which were built by the Great Central Railway.

The simplified schematic in Fig. 271 is different in that there are signal boxes of other companies, mostly of North Eastern Railway origin, that are not shown for clarity but important junctions that are shown even if not necessarily of L&Y origin. The lines nearby are Midland and North Eastern intertwined with the L&Y.

Cutsyke Junction (CJ)

Date Built	1975
LYR Type or Builder	BR North Eastern Region Non Standard
No. of Levers	IFS Panel
Way of Working	TCB
Current Status	Closed
Listed (Y/N)	N

The junction in the title, like so many others, is no more, but it ran from Methley towards Leeds off the Midland Railway past Castleford, which was North Eastern Railway and formed the junction with the present line at Cutsyke nearby. Castleford was a prominent mining town with strong rugby league associations and the saying 'Cas for't cup' meaning the Rugby League Challenge Cup was seldom off the back pages of northern newspapers.

There is nothing remarkable about Cutsyke Junction except that the gates it controls were a particular form of North Eastern Region quirkiness. The original way of opening and closing level crossing gates involved mechanical linkages, often underneath the road, and a gate wheel in the box. If the road was at an angle to the tracks the mechanisms could be extremely complicated to ensure all gates closed at roughly the same time. There are few gate-operated crossings left.

The North Eastern Region of British Railways hit upon the idea of having a motor and wheel attached to the actual gates as shown in Fig. 272; one of the gates is on the left. This idea worked well enough and ensured that substantial gates could still be used rather than flimsy barriers, which is useful in areas where livestock is about. These gates too are being replaced.

The IFS panel that controls all the gate mechanisms has been removed to the National Railway Museum.

Prince of Wales Colliery (P)

Date Built	1912
LYR Type or Builder	L&Y+
No. of Levers	IFS Panel
Way of Working	TCB
Current Status	Active
Listed (Y/N)	N

Fig. 272   Cutsyke Junction signal box, June 2009.

Fig. 273   Prince of Wales Colliery signal box, June 2009.

Fig. 274   Prince of Wales Colliery signal box main line connection and crossover, June 2009.

Network Rail had written a letter in April 2014 advising the train operating companies that the box was to be 'rationalized'. The reason given was that the Prince of Wales Colliery had closed so there was no need for the box any more. A subsequent letter, a month later, withdrew the proposal.

The box seems to be a stayer, at least in the meantime, as it had already survived a fire in 1995.

The colliery, near Pontefract, closed in 2002 and planning permission was granted in 2013 for housing and other domestic facilities, but there is a spoil and slag heap of 3.5 million tonnes that needs to be moved first, and the box seems to be needed for that. Some of the heap is coal that will fuel power stations. Pontefract featured in one of Michael Portillo's *Great Railway Journeys* television programmes made by the BBC.

Fig. 274 shows the crossover and sidings to the former drift mine.

Hensall (H)

Date Built	1875
LYR Type or Builder	Yardley Type 1 (L&Y)
No. of Levers	8, IFS panel
Way of Working	TCB
Current Status	Active
Listed (Y/N)	Y (2013)

Hensall, near Selby and on the way to the former coal-exporting port of Goole, also now controls the movements to and from the massive Drax power station. The power station is fed a mixture of coal and biomass pellets.

The station is listed and preserved, with L&Y cast iron signs as well as Edwardian and 1930s enamel advertising signs.

The station also has two-level platforms – the platform nearest the station house is lower and

Fig. 275   Hensall signal box, June 2008.

therefore earlier than that found further along. Early railway coaches had steps and footboards to enable passengers to reach these lower levels; when platforms were built higher and coaches no longer had footboards and multiple steps, portable platform steps were used at such lower platforms. This meant that train drivers had to pull up with some precision to be near the wooden steps, and alighting in wet weather or snow could be tricky.

Fig. 276 shows the rear of Hensall signal box and a view of the chimney stack, as in later years. The brick-built relay room is not part of the listing. The well-preserved blue wooden platform waiting shelter is a rare beast, as usually these are one of the first things to go whereas the station buildings were usually sold off as dwellings.

Fig. 276   Hensall signal box, rear view and wooden platform waiting shelter, June 2008.

CHAPTER 4

Furness Railway

The Furness Railway built its wealth on the traditional smokestack industries of coal, iron and steel. Shipbuilding was then thrown into this heady mix – some of the heaviest engineering there is – and in addition the line also brought out slate and other minerals.

The railway, at 190 route miles (306km), is one of the smaller constituents of the LMS but today represents a semaphore signal haven, with a few colour light signals and hardly any TCB working. It remains much as it was in the 1960s and the signal boxes are quite different from those of any other company and impressively varied for so small a company.

The line sets off from Carnforth, with its LNWR and MR connections, and makes its way along the

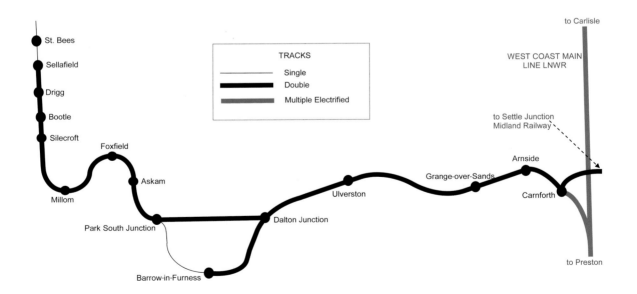

Fig. 277 Furness Railway schematic diagram.

pretty River Kent estuary and Morecambe Bay past the beautiful South Lakes and on to Barrow-in-Furness, which had been the FR's headquarters.

The lines then heads north up the Cumbrian coast past Sellafield nuclear facility to St Bees by single track, and an end-on junction with the former LNWR line from Carlisle at Whitehaven.

Carnforth Station Junction (CS)

Date Built	1903
Furness Type or Builder	Furness Type 4+
No. of Levers	59
Way of Working	TCB, AB
Current Status	Active
Listed (Y/N)	Y

Carnforth was one of the last bastions of steam in 1968 and its loco shed designation of 10A can still be seen on some preserved locomotives running today. The depot remains as the home of West Coast Railways, whom we met at Hellifield on the Midland Railway (*see* Chapter 2).

Carnforth is also well known as the setting for the 1945 David Lean film *Brief Encounter*, written by Noel Coward. There is a museum with some general railway artefacts and a Brief Encounter café, which was popular and atmospheric at the time of the survey. The clock that was seen in the film has been restored and is an example from Joyce of Whitchurch.

The signal box itself is shown in Fig. 278, and straight away the distinctive terracotta roof finials and reinforced brick outhouse style of architecture make the box stand out. The brick structure at the far right-hand end is the staircase.

The lever frame has only lost five levers in its life so the box is doing more or less what it was designed to do although the TCB working to the West Coast Main Line must have had an impact. The box works TCB to Preston power box, AB to Arnside and AB to Settle Junction.

Note that there is a class 47 in what appears to be Network South East livery, Mark 1 BR coaches and the red telephone box as well as the 25kV of the West Coast Main Line spur. Within a quarter-mile

Fig. 278   Carnforth Station Junction signal box, February 2006.

Fig. 279   Carnforth station with original listed signal box, December 2004.

Fig. 280   Carnforth station with 10A engine shed, Midland signal box and West Coast coaches, December 2004.

the electrification ends and it is the Furness main line to Barrow-in-Furness and beyond. There are two yards with run-round loops, one of which is a virtual quarry for ballast, on the right going down the line to Barrow.

The two tracks in front of the box are the Midland Railway line to Settle Junction.

It's two for the price of one with Fig. 279 showing the original Carnforth station signal box, which is so old no one knows exactly how old. The Furness got to Carnforth in 1865 so the box may date from then. It is also listed. The lines on the right are the

Midland Railway to Settle Junction and what looks like a Pacer class 142 is about to set out for there. The West Coast Main Line spur continues past the red colour light signal.

As unlikely as it sounds, it's three for the price of one with the compact and bijou Midland Railway box in West Coast's yard in Fig. 280. This was formerly at Selside, north of Kendal in Cumbria. The former 10A steam shed is the large brick building slightly to the right of the box. Note that there is semaphore signalling in the yard as well as an old gas lamp. The coaches appear to be BR Mark 2s.

Fig. 281   Arnside signal box and the River Kent, October 2014.

Arnside (AE)

Date Built	1903
Furness Type or Builder	Furness Type 4
No. of Levers	35
Way of Working	AB
Current Status	Active
Listed (Y/N)	Y (2013)

Fig. 282   Arnside signal box and platform starter signal, October 2014.

Carnforth was a start but we get properly into the Cumbrian countryside at Arnside. Arnside is a village that faces the estuary of the River Kent on the northeastern corner of Morecambe Bay. The location has been awarded Area of Outstanding Natural Beauty status.

The Arnside viaduct, over a quarter-mile (400m) long, over the River Kent, is just beyond the signal that has its back to us in Fig. 281. The box is a stone structure and even has a stone staircase. All that is missing from the chimney stack is the pot. The eight-digit number on the signal post is to advise drivers to call the local signaller if required on the GSM-R network. This uses digital mobile phone technology so speech and SMS messages are featured. It would appear to draw the line at social media and internet shopping.

Fig. 282 is looking back towards Carnforth, and a train is expected on the down side towards Barrow. The station platform ramp on the up side can just be seen. There are London Midland Region enamel name plates at both ends of the box.

Arnside station is very well kept in Fig. 283, with tubs of flowers and an autumn planting, as well as a neat and tidy appearance overall. The fine footbridge makes a frame for the line back towards Carnforth.

Grange-over-Sands (GS)

Date Built	1956
Furness Type or Builder	BR London Midland Region
No. of Levers	25
Way of Working	AB
Current Status	Active
Listed (Y/N)	N

Before the coming of the railway, Grange-over-Sands was a fishing village but then developed into a delightfully pretty Victorian resort with a mile-long promenade. There were health spa facilities with a very early sanatorium as well as spring water.

The village is opposite Morecambe Bay, which used to be the principal access point for Grange-over-Sands before the railway.

Grange-over-Sands signal box (Fig. 284) is the first and last box on this railway that is not Furness Railway in origin. Of all the boxes covered so far, many have rearward-facing windows but this box has none. Perhaps the signaller wouldn't pass many trains, being too busy looking at the view.

The signal box has only a trailing crossover with attendant ground discs for reversing moves,

Fig. 283   Arnside station and platform starter signal, October 2014.

Fig. 284 *Grange-over-Sands signal box and Morecambe Bay, October 2014.*

Fig. 285 *Grange-over-Sands signal box looking towards Carnforth, October 2014.*

as shown in Fig. 285. The rocky and hilly terrain means that the railway follows the estuary of the River Kent very closely, and right behind the box is the promenade and then the sands. The view is looking back towards Arnside and Carnforth. The box is 9 miles 31 chains (15.1km) from Carnforth.

Fig. 286 shows Grange-over-Sands station, looking towards Ulverston, with the promenade on the left. The sturdy stone-built station is complete with all facilities and all still in railway use. The station won the 'Heritage Station of the Year' award in 2012. The box is behind the camera.

The stone-built goods shed is on the right, just by the up platform 1 ramp. It is now a garage and the former goods yard has a number of small businesses there.

Ulverston (UN)

Date Built	1900
Furness Type or Builder	Furness 4+
No. of Levers	22
Way of Working	AB
Current Status	Active
Listed (Y/N)	N

Ulverston is a charming town and a centre for South Lakes tourism. It boasts the deepest, widest and shortest canal in the Britain at 1¼ miles (2km), which was once a factor in Ulverston's economy. It is also the birthplace of Stan Laurel of Laurel and Hardy fame and there is a museum to the pair in the town.

Fig. 286 *Grange-over-Sands station and goods shed from the promenade, October 2014.*

Fig. 287 *Ulverston signal box and the view towards Barrow-in-Furness, October 2014.*

Fig. 288 *Ulverston station looking towards Carnforth, October 2014.*

Fig. 287 is looking towards Dalton Junction, and the lines that needed to splay out to go round the platform on the station are becoming parallel again. The station is behind the camera. The starter signal is pulled off for a class 150 heading for Barrow; the use of whitewash as a sighting board is in evidence here but the practice has been largely discontinued elsewhere. The former goods yard is accessed by the trailing crossover, and there is a point after the crossover into what is now a permanent way depot. The headshunt seems to be out of use, with the octagonal stop sign and flashing beacon above it. Note that the bracket signal is cantilevered out across the track to enable trains coming from Dalton Junction to see it earlier. The box has been modernized to a degree with add-on toilet block and a steel cage.

Fig. 288 shows Ulverston station with the signal box behind the camera, and it is a temple of opulence in stone with an impressive clock tower and supporting buildings. The canopies on the island platform used to extend to where the camera is but at least the supports have been retained and used for lighting. A platform with two faces, as platform 1 has on the right, usually means busy trains with lots of passengers alighting here.

The starter for the line to Carnforth can just be seen under the canopy on the left.

Fig. 289 is looking in the Ulverston station direction. The box originally had forty levers when the branch line to Lakeside was in being. This station of Lakeside was the interchange for the Windermere steamers, and this facility remains with the Lakeside and Haverthwaite Railway preserved

Fig. 289   Ulverston signal box crossover and bracket signal for siding, October 2014.

Fig. 290   Dalton Junction signal box, October 2014.

steam railway. They have a couple of preserved Furness Railway signal boxes as well as stations and a delightfully scenic run.

Ulverston signal box is 19 miles and 47 chains (31.5km) from Carnforth. The box is provided with a switch so can be bypassed if required.

Dalton Junction (DJ)

Date Built	1902
Furness Type or Builder	Furness 4+
No. of Levers	20
Way of Working	AB
Current Status	Active
Listed (Y/N)	N

Dalton-in-Furness is mentioned in the Domesday Book and was the historic capital of Furness. This interesting town also has a castle and safari park zoo as main tourist attractions. The ruins of Dalton Abbey are a little way out of the town but it was the largest Cistercian monastery in the country after Fountains Abbey in Yorkshire. It did not survive the reign of Henry VIII unscathed.

Dalton Junction signal box, however, is surviving pretty much unscathed, and exists in splendid isolation although Barrow-in-Furness is close by. The box is fairly original (Fig. 290) except for security wire mesh on the modernized windows and blocked-up locking frame windows.

Dalton Junction's track layout and signal box can be seen in operation in Fig. 291, with a class

142 Pacer unit coming from Barrow-in-Furness and heading for Carnforth. The other tracks go to Park South Junction and on towards Sellafield. Note that there is a facing-point lock between the tracks on the line leading down to Park South on the left of the Pacer.

Looking at Dalton Junction from the side and rear in Fig. 292, you can see an extremely robust iron bracket above the locking frame window aperture. Perhaps this is bolted to the frame to stop either the frame or box wall from going anywhere. Of note is the use of stone blocks to build up a walkway round the box, which is perched on the embankment.

The box interior is shown in Fig. 293 and the diagram shows the tracks from Ulverston, on the

Fig. 291   Dalton Junction signal box and class 142 heading for Carnforth, October 2014.

Fig. 292 *Rear view of Dalton Junction signal box, November 2006.*

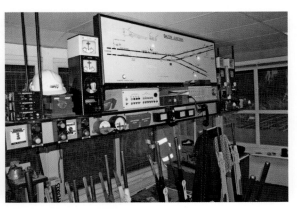

Fig. 293 *Dalton Junction signal box interior with diagram and block shelf, November 2006.*

left, leading to the trailing crossover, and Barrow branching upwards and Park South downwards.

The three BR domino absolute block instruments are on the block shelf, one for each direction, and each has a Welwyn Release beneath it. The block switch is on the left underneath the Network Rail hard hat. To the left of the block switch are training protection and warning system (TPWS) power supply status indicators and control units.

There are mostly colour light signals, and their status is reflected by the black rectangular units screwed to the front of the block shelf with the coloured lights. There is still one semaphore home signal, however, and its status indicator is on the block shelf next to the lever collars coloured red and marked 'Engineering Work'. The signal is no. 5 and it is shown on the diagram in Fig. 295.

The frame at Dalton Junction (Fig. 294) has only four spare white levers, and the levers reversed are the facing-point lock (lever 8) and branch to Park South point. This was the point referred to in Fig. 291 although it is not shown reversed in that view

as it is some years later. Of interest is the carefully painted board at the rear of the frame describing the individual lever functions.

Finally at Dalton Junction, in Fig. 295, is the right-hand end of the diagram and AB instruments. The semaphore signal referred to above with its circular status indicator is signal 5 on the diagram on the way to Park South. All four colour light signals on the diagram are on, or at danger, as we can see by their status indicators on the front of the block shelf.

The left-hand block instrument for Barrow-in-Furness is showing Line Clear and that has been selected by the signaller at Dalton Junction. That indication will be repeated at Barrow signal box to inform the signaller it is safe to send the train. The train is on its way from Barrow but not in Dalton

Fig. 294 *Dalton Junction signal box interior with lever frame, November 2006.*

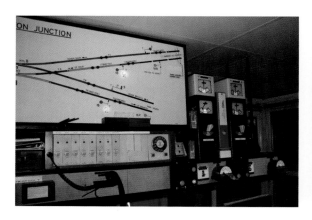

Fig. 295   Dalton Junction signal box interior diagram with track circuit detail and absolute block instruments, November 2006.

Fig. 296   Barrow-in-Furness signal box, October 2014.

Junction's section yet otherwise the AB instrument would show Train on Line. The signaller would give the Train out of Section bell code to Dalton to signify this. The signaller at Dalton then selects Train on Line on that instrument, which is then mirrored back to Barrow. Track circuits give a remote indication and they are the double lights in the different-coloured track sections on the diagram.

The track circuits tell us that the train is not in the section anyway. Note the miniature telephone exchange on the block shelf.

From Dalton Junction we are taking the line to Barrow-in-Furness.

Barrow-in-Furness (BF)

Date Built	1907
Furness Type or Builder	Furness 4
No. of Levers	67
Way of Working	AB, TB
Current Status	Active
Listed (Y/N)	N

Barrow-in-Furness has long been associated with shipbuilding and so it continues to this day. It is also the only place in Britain where submarines are built. The Trident nuclear boats were all built in the

Devonshire Dock Hall and the Astute class attack submarines are also being built there. The yard builds surface ships too, with the HMS *Bulwark* landing support and helicopter carrier being a noteworthy example; HMS *Bulwark* is currently the Royal Navy's flagship. It is also the only shipyard in Britain able to carry out work on nuclear facilities. The foreign uranium fuel rods sent for re-processing at Sellafield are landed at the Port of Barrow in specially protected ships. Fuel rods from all over Britain go past Dalton Junction and Park South Junction to Sellafield.

Barrow-in-Furness signal box survived almost unscathed for over 100 years and that included a blitzkrieg on the station nearby in May 1941, when the station was almost completely destroyed. There is a memorial in the station to those who died in FR service in World War I as well as in the Blitz in World War II.

It had been after the style of Ulverston station with an overall roof so was quite a pretty sight. It is not surprising the locking frame windows were bricked up and a bit of one of the finials is missing (Fig. 296). A sympathetic addition is the amenity block at the rear, even down to matching terracotta ridge tiles.

Barrow-in-Furness station platforms and signalling are shown in Fig. 297. The platforms number 1,

2, 3 from left to right. Signalled out of the bay platform 3 is a train for Askam and Carlisle. Although tracks run from platforms 1 and 2 it soon goes into single track and the working to Park South Junction from here is tokenless block. This uses special block instruments that lock any opposing move when a move in one direction is selected and accepted by the receiving box. The facing point out of platform 1 is to the carriage sidings, which are still in use; a class 150 two-car unit is in the sidings, with its red tail light showing.

The station is signalled bi-directionally and the subsidiary signal on platform 2 has a stencil box-type route indicator to the right of the signal arm to clarify which route is being taken – the platform 1 loop over the crossover or over the crossover and into the carriage sidings. Although this is not a single line at this point, single lines are always signalled bi-directionally. Note that there are anti-climb boards on the signal ladders. On platform 1 is a yellow push button that has to be held in for 10 seconds to signify to the box that the train has arrived complete with a tail lamp, as the signaller would not be able to observe that normally. It looked disused.

Fig. 298 shows Barrow-in-Furness station looking towards Dalton Junction and Carnforth. The platforms are of solid stone and seem to be settling down for another 150 years. The track work doesn't seem so sure, although this is a telephoto shot.

With what looks like limestone quarrying as a backdrop, a Northern Trains class 150 makes its way out of the bay platform 3 towards Askam and Carlisle in Fig. 299. The bracket signal is for platforms 2 and 3 with the lower for platform 3, as that signifies a lower speed. The subsidiary arms below must be calling on arms as we saw at Blackpool North in Chapter 3. The train is moving past a triple-decker ground disc, which would signal a reversing move into any of the platforms.

Fig. 300 takes a closer look at the carriage sidings. The far siding is a refuelling point. The sidings are all loops that meet at a headshunt or run round so there is no exit from the sidings at the other end of

Fig. 297 Barrow-in-Furness station starter and subsidiary signals, Park South end, October 2014.

Fig. 298 Barrow-in-Furness station starter signals, Carnforth end, October 2014.

Fig. 299 Barrow-in-Furness, and a class 150 departs for the single line and Park South Junction, October 2014.

Fig. 300   Barrow-in-Furness station carriage sidings, washery and refuelling point, with a class 150 in attendance, October 2014.

Fig. 301   Park South signal box and garden shed, November 2006.

the facility. This arrangement is not used so much these days as almost all trains are double-ended multiple unit types.

This partially accounts for the ground discs that signal movement back into the platforms. Note the facing-point lock on the first point out of platform 1, which is interlocked locally with the ground discs so that it is impossible to pull a disc off unless the exit point is changed over correctly and locked. This local interlocking is referred to as 'slide detection'. In the box the facing-point lock lever would also be interlocked with other signals on the frame itself. The rusty track running off camera shot to the left is to a double platform bay. There were at least six platforms at the original Barrow station.

Barrow station is 28 miles 76 chains (46.6km) from Carnforth.

Park South (PS)

Date Built	1883
Furness Type or Builder	Furness 3
No. of Levers	24
Way of Working	TB, AB
Current Status	Active
Listed (Y/N)	N

Park South (Fig. 301) even has a chimney pot in its list of heritage credentials even though the windows and stairs are modernized items. The stone citadel style of architecture is typical Furness Railway.

The signaller, as with many others, is a keen gardener judging by the mini garden at the front of the relay room and the hanging baskets and planter tubs. The garden shed is a feature not often found, but there will need to be a place to nurture seedlings as well as store gardening equipment. Tomatoes used to be a commonly grown crop but seem to be less favoured in recent years.

There is only one name plate; the left-hand end example is missing.

Park South is often referred to as a junction and this is shown in Fig. 302. The route is set for a train to Barrow-in-Furness station from the Askam and Carlisle direction. The class 150 departure in the section on Barrow, above, would have come off the junction towards the camera, except on the right-hand track towards Askam and Carlisle.

Park South and Dalton Junction are the only two boxes on the line to have an appreciable number of colour light signals, and as we can see from the block shelf at Park South in Fig. 303, it is a mix of both types. Some of the colour lights are associated with the tokenless block way of working the single line to Barrow.

The track layout with junction can be clearly seen on the diagram.

The block instrument and the near end is to Askam and there is a train in section. The diagram bears this out, as there is a pair of red lights denoting an occupied track section and the train has come from the Askam direction.

As this is autumn, the signaller has a good display of house plants to compensate.

Fig. 304 shows the frame, where fifteen of the twenty-four levers are unused. A facing point and a point lever are reversed, though. The lever painted blue and black is a point and facing-point lock combined. Non-lever-operated points usually have the locking mechanism integral to the unit and so only one lever is actually required. Points can be electrically or hydraulically operated, as well as by levers.

Back up to the block shelf, and the reason that none of the signal levers are reversed when there is a train in section becomes clear in Fig. 305. Some of the signals can be switched to automatic mode, as we can see by the switch on the block shelf relating to signal 18R (remote), which is the down line from Askam's distant, bottom far right of the picture. It is also bottom right on the diagram.

The signaller has accepted a train from Askam and the domino block instrument has been selected here to be Train on Line by Park South. The block bell and tapper key for the bell codes are integral and at the bottom of the instrument.

The previous figure dealt with where the train had come from, and in Fig. 306 we can see where it is going. It cannot be to Dalton Junction as there is nothing on the block for the larger domino instrument. It can only be on the single line to Barrow with the tokenless block (TB) instrument right on the left-hand end of the block shelf. The TB instrument has three positions and they are, from left to right, Normal (line blocked), Train in Section and Train Accepted.

The white switch can select either Normal or Accept. Below that on the block shelf are two push switches, Offer and Train Arrived. Barrow signal box has the same there. To pass the train from Askam to Barrow the signaller at Park South

Fig. 302   Park South with the single track to Barrow-in-Furness on the right, November 2006.

Fig. 303   Park South signal box interior with diagram and block shelf, November 2006.

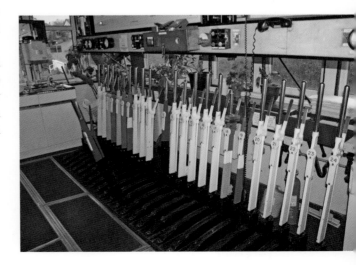

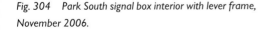

Fig. 304   Park South signal box interior with lever frame, November 2006.

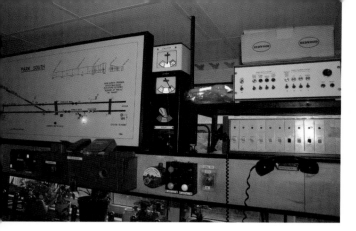

Fig. 305   Park South signal box interior with Askam absolute block instrument and track circuit detail on the diagram, November 2006.

Fig. 306   Park South signal box interior with absolute block instrument and tokenless block instrument, November 2006.

presses the Offer button, and if Barrow selects Accept, this is reflected on Park South's TB instrument as Train Accepted. This then locks all the signals on the single line from Barrow to Park South

at danger. In other words, a train cannot pass in the opposite direction to the one this train is going unless it passes several signals at danger. When the train has arrived in the section at Park South the track circuits sense this and turn both block instruments at Park South and Barrow to Train in Section.

When the train has arrived at Barrow, complete with tail lamp, the signaller at Barrow selects Train Arrived and the instruments revert to Normal. This operation is interlocked with any relevant points on the route.

In this process our train from Askam is Train in Section and we have already confirmed this from the track circuit.

Fig. 307 shows the train, in the shape of a class 150, heading for the junction, which can just be seen in the distance, and Barrow-in-Furness. Park South also supervises a couple of road crossings.

Finally at Park South, Fig. 308 was initially taken for the distant signal adjuster wheel, which is the large black object screwed to the floor with two gear wheels and a hand knob on the top. This is to take up the slack in hot weather caused by the expansion of signal wires. This effect can mean a signal does not come fully off when pulled, which could affect whether any trains can run through the interlocking. If the signal is not fully off the next signal could not be pulled off and so on.

However, there is more. The stop plates on signals 3 and 4 are a reminder that these signals are in automatic mode and these levers are not to be pulled while automatic is selected. The signaller must be able to override automatic mode if that system should fail, which is why there is still a lever there.

The ivorine plates on the signal are a reminder of which levers have to be pulled first before this lever

Fig. 307   Park South signal box interior and a class 150 to take the single line to Barrow-in-Furness, November 2006.

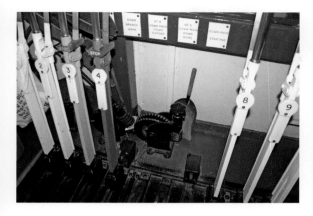

Fig. 308   Park South signal box interior with signal wire adjuster and lever frame detail, November 2006.

can be pulled due to the interlocking in the frame. With signal 3 it is levers 4 and 7. The ivorine plates on the wall describe the lever functions (like the painted board we saw at Dalton Junction).

Askam (AM)

Date Built	1890
Furness Type or Builder	Furness 2
No. of Levers	22
Way of Working	AB
Current Status	Active
Listed (Y/N)	Y

Askam signal box (Fig. 309) is possibly the most original box on the line, complete with chimney pot, though there are other contenders. The windows and steps are modernized, and usually with listed buildings permission would be sought for any external changes. The Furness Railway seems to have attracted the attention of English Heritage out of all proportion to the total number of boxes involved but it is an enclave of railway history in many ways.

If Askam station isn't listed perhaps it should be (Fig. 310). Paley and Austin, the architects of this station, crop up time and again on the Furness Railway. This chalet style is attractive and extends across to the waiting shelter on the up platform towards Barrow, although that is brick-built rather than stone. The view is looking towards Park South and Barrow. The station originally transported iron ore, locally mined, to Barrow and Millom.

Fig. 311 shows Askam station looking towards Foxfield and Carlisle. The trailing crossover pair are the only points in the layout and the box controlled the crossing barriers manually at the survey date. If the platforms at your station are too long for the two-car class 150s on the route, why not convert the unwanted length into lawn? Provided it's kept tidy it can be an asset.

Note the period platform edging slabs.

Fig. 309   Askam signal box, November 2006.

Fig. 310   Askam signal box and station building, November 2006.

Fig. 311   Askam station with the view towards Foxfield and Carlisle, November 2006.

Foxfield

Date Built	*c.*1879
Furness Type or Builder	Furness 3+
No. of Levers	52
Way of Working	AB
Current Status	Active
Listed (Y/N)	N

Foxfield, in Fig. 312, was a junction to Broughton-in-Furness to tap the local copper mines and to Coniston for Lake Coniston. It made a connection with the Lake Coniston steamers and was very popular for many years until it succumbed to road competition and closed in 1962. The frame of the Park South signal box is from Coniston signal box originally so some part of the branch lives on.

As with all junction stations there was a sizeable goods yard for traffic interchanges. This is where the mountain and coastal scenery starts.

Foxfield is one of the few places where the signal box is combined with the station building. There is another example on Anglesey in LNWR territory.

There are no points here now so many of the fifty-two levers must be painted white.

There is no footbridge here – passengers cross the tracks under supervision of the signaller.

Fig. 313 shows Foxfield box and station waiting room looking towards Millom and Carlisle. The station house is on the right behind the station running-in board, and is in private hands now. The steam age water tower and tank are on the right also. If a water supply could not be obtained from a local spring it had to be pumped, sometimes by static steam engine, into the tank. The tanks were

Fig. 312   Foxfield signal box and station building, November 2006.

Fig. 313   Foxfield signal box and station building and water tower, with the view towards Carlisle, November 2006.

Fig. 314   Foxfield station platform looking back to Askam, November 2006.

always elevated to give a head or pressure of water so that loco tanks would be replenished by gravity.

Fig. 314 shows Foxfield station island platform and the view looking back towards Askam. The bracket signal had more than one doll or post on it at one time and there were rusty rails opposite the platform on the right. The platform, unlike Askam, needs mowing.

Millom

Date Built	1891
Furness Type or Builder	Furness 1+
No. of Levers	30
Way of Working	AB
Current Status	Active
Listed (Y/N)	N

Millom is a town founded on iron ore and the ability of the Furness Railway to transport it. Although there was a collection of villages here dating from the Domesday Book, the town was a product of the Industrial Revolution. Like so many others, it has had to adapt, post heavy industry, and activities such as tourism and leisure have taken over to some extent. The town is a centre of amateur rugby league and perhaps that reflects the gritty character of the people who have had to adapt to change.

Millom signal box (Fig. 315) is yet another Furness Railway variation, although heavily modernized. The layout here is a trailing crossover and a siding on the down side towards Carlisle with a

Fig. 315   Millom signal box, November 2006.

headshunt. The box was hit by a train and demolished in 1913 but rebuilt within a few months.

Millom station is shown in Fig. 316, looking towards Foxfield. The down siding is on the right and there were once more here, including a goods yard. Builder's merchants seem to make a habit of occupying former goods yards. The platforms are recent and longer than the two-car class 150s that mostly ply this route. Note the abutments on the stone wall on the far right – there was an overall roof here at one time – the original footbridge and the distinctive roof finials on the station building.

Looking towards Carlisle in Fig. 317, the trailing crossover and siding are clearly visible off the main line. The box is behind the right-hand bridge pillar, which has an office of some sort in it. You can just

Fig. 316   Millom station and siding towards Foxfield, November 2006.

see the FR initials in the wrought iron tracery work on the platform canopy.

Millow station is 45 miles 1 chain (72.4km) from Carnforth.

Silecroft (SC)

Date Built	1923
Furness Type or Builder	Furness 4
No. of Levers	15
Way of Working	AB
Current Status	Active
Listed (Y/N)	N

Silecroft is a village located on the coast at the extreme end of the Lake District National Park. The village is near Black Combe, which, at almost 2,000ft (600m), dominates the area. The location is popular with holidaymakers and tourists with its sandy beach and mountainous scenery.

Silecroft signal box (Fig. 318) was built in LMS days so does not have the age of some of its neighbours. However, some of the track thereabouts has bullhead rail, which reinforces the period feel. Here is another chimney that is stacked out and topped with a pot and it feels as if the branch goods loco is going to leave a few big bits of coal for the signal box fireplace. The sign on the locking frame room door underneath the steps proclaims 'ACCESS S&T STAFF ONLY' where S&T are Signal and Telegraph.

Fig. 319 is looking back towards Millom and a home and distant signal on the same post down the line. The trailing crossover is the only set of points here. Note that there are extended point frog wing rails that seem to act as check rails when the crossover is reversed.

Nothing of Silecroft station (Fig. 320) has survived except a massive stone goods shed that is not now rail connected. Note that the platforms were originally quite low and have been built up with

Fig. 317   Millom station looking towards Carlisle, November 2006.

Fig. 318   Silecroft signal box, November 2006.

Fig. 319   Silecroft with the view to Millom, November 2006.

Fig. 320   Silecroft with the view to Carlisle, November 2006.

courses of bricks but the now unused parts are still at the original height. There's a colour light signal on the right hand platform.

Silecroft station is 48 miles 16 chains (77.6km) from Carnforth.

Bootle (BE)

Date Built	c.1871
Furness Type or Builder	Furness 1+
No. of Levers	15
Way of Working	AB
Current Status	Active
Listed (Y/N)	Y (2013)

Fig. 321   Bootle signal box, November 2006.

Bootle's origins are medieval and the signal box almost similarly ancient. This pretty village relies on tourism and holidaymakers attracted to its position in the Lake District National Park.

The station is at Hycemoor, a hamlet just outside Bootle.

It is said that the box (Fig. 321) was built in preparation for the line's doubling in 1876. Manual gates are at the crossing here and there is an interlock with signals. The signaller appears to be another gardener, and this is reflected all over the station.

Bootle station, a solid Victorian stone station building, is on the right in Fig. 322, with period wooden waiting shelter on the opposite platform. A monolithic stone goods shed is past the crossing

Fig. 322   Bootle station, signal box and goods shed looking towards Carlisle, November 2006.

Fig. 323   Bootle station looking
towards Silecroft, November 2006.

on the right. This view is towards Carlisle. Bootle station is 53 miles 34 chains (86km) from Carnforth.

The privately owned station building on the right in Fig. 323 extends down the platform. The waiting shelter on the opposite platform has its share of planters and tubs. The small green building on the right is a lamp oil store, and it is remarkable in 2006 that lamps were still lit by oil. You can see the benefit to a driver of the whitewashed bridge for the home signal, on the way to Silecroft.

Drigg (DG)

Date Built	*c.*1871
Furness Type or Builder	Furness 1+
No. of Levers	14
Way of Working	AB
Current Status	Active
Listed (Y/N)	N

Drigg was home to an explosives factory in World War II, and this site has been converted into a repository for low-level nuclear waste. There is a siding with two loops and a run-round to service this facility. The waste consists of items such as clothing and tools and is strictly controlled.

Just south of Drigg is the Ravenglass and Eskdale steam railway, which is a preserved line for tourists but originally was built to bring haematite iron ore from quarries near Boot, 7 miles (11km) inland. The line is very picturesque and the route formed a favourite part of one of Wainwright's Walks. It was originally 3-foot gauge but was converted in 1913 to be 15-inch gauge.

The box shown in Fig. 324 has been heavily plasticized and modernized, which perhaps was a factor in Bootle being listed when the similar Furness Type 1 box at Drigg was not.

Drigg station, similar to Bootle, complete with goods shed and manually operated gates, is shown

Fig. 324   Drigg signal box, November 2006.

Fig. 325   Drigg station and goods shed, November 2006.

in Fig. 325. There was a coffee and craft shop in the station building at the survey date.

The platforms don't look as low in Fig. 326 as some others at Drigg station, but someone has thoughtfully provided steps for passengers. Drigg is spelled out in painted stones and, together with small gardens around them, this used to be quite a common feature at country stations. The ground disc is for the trailing crossover reversal moves past the box.

Fig. 326 Drigg station crossing with platform steps, November 2006.

Sellafield (SD)

Date Built	1918
Furness Type or Builder	Furness 4
No. of Levers	49
Way of Working	AB, KT
Current Status	Active
Listed (Y/N)	N

Sellafield and nearby Seascale will always be welded into the British consciousness as early venues for the nuclear industry, as they still are today. Nuclear flask trains come from all over Britain in the care of Direct Rail Services centred at Crewe, and special ships transport enriched uranium rods for export and import spent rods for enrichment at the Port of Barrow. The cargo is then transported to Sellafield in flasks by rail. After Sellafield the remainder of the Furness Railway to St Bees is single track, which is worked by key token. For an explanation of this way of working, *see* the section on Great Rocks Junction in Chapter 3.

Fig. 327 Sellafield signal box, November 2006.

Fig. 328 Sellafield looking towards St Bees and the single line, November 2006.

Sellafield box has been modernized more than most but the steam age water crane in Fig. 327 just looks as though it needs a leather bag to start work again. The double track from Drigg ends just before the other end of the station here. The ends of the station platforms ramp ends are just visible. The line on the right has two platform faces, an indication of the large number of people arriving here by train to go to work at Sellafield. The line continues to St Bees in the depicted direction as single track.

Fig. 328 shows the line continuing under the road bridge and then curving round onto the

Fig. 329   Sellafield looking towards Drigg and the nuclear installations, November 2006.

Fig. 330   Sellafield station looking towards St Bees, November 2006.

single line to St Bees. The siding straight on is the up refuge siding with just a ground disc as an exit signal. The tracks are set for the line to St Bees and Carlisle.

Fig. 329 is looking back towards Drigg and the facilities provided for the nuclear industry. There are two loops and five sidings with a headshunt. Note that the two home signals are tied together with a steel support. Sellafield must be about the only place on Network Rail with two steam age water cranes.

Fig. 330 shows Sellafield station, where the niceties of heritage buildings have been blotted out to some extent by the need to shelter lots of passengers and get them between platforms. The original buildings look as though they are from the same stable as Bootle and Drigg.

Sellafield station is 63 miles 72 chains (102.8km) from Carnforth.

St Bees (SB)

Date Built	1891
Furness Type or Builder	Furness 3+
No. of Levers	24
Way of Working	KT
Current Status	Active
Listed (Y/N)	Y (2013)

St Bees is the site of the only mainland cliffs between Wales and Scotland and has a prominent lighthouse to warn shipping of it. The area is one of outstanding beauty and the seabird colony is the largest in north-west England and enjoys SSSI status.

The village dates from medieval times with a priory and many fine buildings. It exported large amounts of sandstone up until 1970 – Barrow-in-Furness station was built with St Bees sandstone.

St Bees signal box (Fig. 331) is yet another Furness Railway listed building and looks as though the next 125 years will follow in the same vein as the last. It works key token back to Sellafield and the same onwards towards Whitehaven at Bransty signal box, but that is in LNWR territory and so will have to wait for Volume 2 of this book. The border between the two railways is about another 3 miles (5km) north and Carlisle is about another 42 miles (68km) from there.

St Bees station with the box at the end of the left-hand platform is shown in Fig. 332. There's a redoubtable stone station building on the right and what looks like a wooden waiting shelter on the left-hand side that has been converted into a bungalow.

Passenger steps that are used to board trains from the low platforms are on the right-hand platform near the footbridge end. The line reverts to single track just beyond the second home signal. The home signal with its back to us is guarding the entry to the loop beyond the loop point. The view is looking towards Whitehaven and Carlisle.

Fig. 333 is looking the other way back towards Sellafield, and the loop closes pretty soon after the

Fig. 331   St Bees signal box, November 2006.

Fig. 332   St Bees station and signal box looking towards Whitehaven and Carlisle, November 2006.

platforms but with a headshunt or trap point at this end. The elevated ground disc to enable better sighting is common on the former GWR lines but rare around here.

St Bees station is 70 miles 18 chains (113km) from Carnforth.

Fig. 333   St Bees station looking towards Sellafield, November 2006.

Fig. 334   Rear of St Bees signal box, November 2006.

CHAPTER 5

Glasgow and South Western Railway

The Glasgow and South Western Railway (G&SWR) was a considerable undertaking, with 1,128 route miles (1,815km) in a rectangle of land formed by Glasgow, Ayr, Stranraer and Carlisle. The railway covered most of Ayrshire and what is now the county of Dumfries and Galloway. The railway runs through spectacular mountain and coastal scenery.

The network extended beyond railways, with a sizeable holding in shipping to service the ports of Ardrossan, Greenock, Stranraer and Troon as well as Clyde steamer bases.

The Ayrshire coal field was a major customer for the line and the coal connection continues with the substantial import of coal through Hunterston in Ayrshire and the carriage by rail to power stations in England. We have seen some of this traffic on the Settle–Carlisle Line of the Midland Railway.

The G&SWR formed an alliance with the Midland Railway, and the G&SWR's terminus in Glasgow was at St Enoch's, now long gone. Passenger services now are centred on Central station.

Glasgow is world famous for shipbuilding and heavy industry and it suffered more than most cities in Europe when these activities switched to the Far East. However, it remains a beautiful city with a fine cultural heritage with the likes of Charles Rennie Mackintosh's Glasgow School of Art. Lord Kelvin, an eminent physicist, has a temperature scale named after him. The Glaswegian sense of humour has travelled far and wide with comedians such as Billy Connolly and Kevin Bridges.

Glasgow, in common with other major cities, has been extensively modernized and has no mechanical signalling. However, two lines live on that have some very rare survivors in the ways of working. The resurgence in rail travel probably means that these will disappear soon.

Ayr to Stanraer Harbour

Ayr has long been famous as Glasgow's seaside resort with its sandy beach, racecourse and mild Gulf Stream climate. In later years Ayr attracted holidaymakers from far and wide with the Butlin's Holiday Camp, which survives today in a different format. Ayr was also a commuter base for Glasgow.

As usual the journey begins some way out of Ayr and this line is completely single track from the first signal box; all the boxes are passing places.

Kilkerran (KK)

Date Built	1895
G&SW Type or Builder	G&SW Type 3
No. of Levers	20
Way of Working	TB
Current Status	Active
Listed Scottish Heritage (Y/N)	N

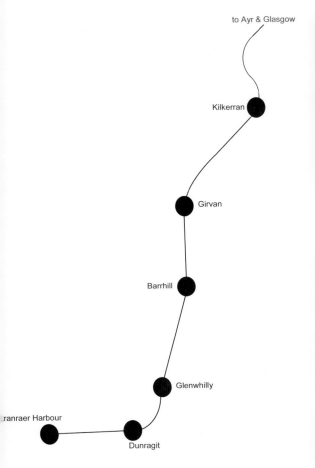

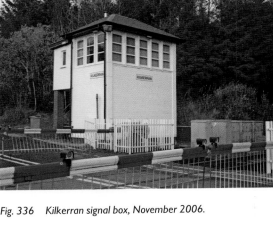

Fig. 336   Kilkerran signal box, November 2006.

Fig. 335   Ayr–Stranraer schematic diagram.

Fig. 337   Kilkerran station, goods shed and approach signals, November 2006.

Kilkerran lost its station in 1965 but the station building survives. The box has had a substantial admin block built on the rear of the box (Fig. 336). Most G&SWR boxes feature timber cladding and a tall structure mindful of sighting needs. The crossing was manually controlled from within the box at the survey date.

Kilkerran station building and goods shed (Fig. 337) remain out of railway service. The bracket signal controls entry into the passing loop.

Kilkerran signal box diagram is shown in Fig. 338, and we can see that although the loop proximity

signals are semaphore, the more outlying signals are colour lights. The different colour tracks define each track circuit and we can see that the box interfaces to the Paisley signalling centre on the outskirts of Glasgow to the north and Girvan to the south. Instead of the colour light signals' aspect being shown on the signal image itself, there are groups of coloured lights below the track part of the diagram with on and off labels. All signals are shown on, or at danger, which is the default condition. The blue-grey box to the right of the diagram is the Scottish

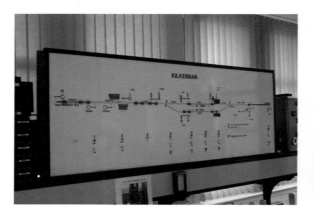

Fig. 338 *Kilkerran signal box interior and diagram, November 2006.*

Fig. 339 *Kilkerran signal box interior and lever frame, November 2006.*

tokenless block instrument and the working of this is covered later in this chapter under Lugton in the Glasgow–Gretna section. Briefly though, tokenless block is a means of single-line working where the instruments provide the locking instead of a token or tablet. This enables trains to proceed without having to stop to exchange tokens.

Kilkerran signal box frame is shown in Fig. 339. The smaller levers are those operated electrically but may still have mechanical interlocking in the frame. The micro switches that control the function can be seen, with their associated wiring, at the base of each cut-down lever. The panel to control the barriers is on the right, by the window.

Mileages to Kilkerran are calculated from the former Bridge Street station, Glasgow, even though that station is disused. The mileage is 53 miles 76 chains (86.8km).

Girvan (GV)

Date Built	c.1893
G&SW Type or Builder	G&SW Type 3
No. of Levers	30
Way of Working	TB, ETT
Current Status	Active
Listed Scottish Heritage (Y/N)	Y (Category B)

Girvan was once a fishing port and is now a small beach resort but with impressive mountain views thrown in. The station is an art deco delight and possibly describable as post-war Odeon style although it was based on the LMS 1930s style. The station was not completed until 1951, five years after the original building burnt down.

The box works TB to Kilkerran and ETT, or electric train tablet, to Barrhill. ETT is a variation on key token, although older and rarer. The driver is issued with a tablet in a hooped pouch as the authority to proceed. The action of removing the token to give to the driver locks the token instrument at the other

Fig. 340 *Girvan signal box, November 2006.*

Fig. 341   Girvan signal box and art deco station, November 2006.

end of the section and prevents a conflicting signalling move being implemented. The release of the tablet enables section signals to be released. The system is locked until either a tablet is placed in the instrument at the end of the section or in the original tablet instrument. There are only three sections of ETT working on Network Rail, all on this line.

Girvan signal box, in Fig. 340, has no name plate, which usually means the next stop is redundancy, but this box is alive and well and still controlling the layout at Girvan except for one small part. The signal box is standing on the original lower platform. Note that the aperture in the platform face for the point rodding has been boarded up and all points must be power operated except for the ground frame shown in Fig. 342.

Fig. 341 is a fine view of Girvan station, signal box and mountains, looking towards Kilkerran and Ayr. The loops appear to be bi-directionally signalled, although the diagram is labelled up and down. Girvan was originally a junction and it is from this historic but absent junction that mileages

are now calculated. There is a milepost at the station with '0' on it.

The view in Fig. 342 is the Kilkerran end of the loop and the up siding, which has its own ground frame to operate the points. Note that the ground frame, on the bottom right of the picture, has a blue facing-point lock lever, which means trains carrying passengers can cross over it; this is slightly strange as it is described as an engineer's siding. The box is right by the ground frame, which again is odd but the layout must have changed here over the years because the box was first known as 'Girvan Station', then 'Girvan No. 3' and finally 'Girvan No. 2' before its present designation. The semaphore signal that is off is for the platform that the camera is on. The loop signal is of the lattice-post type, and while they are still fairly common

Fig. 342   Girvan station, ground frame and signals looking towards Kilkerran, November 2006.

in Scotland they are unknown in the rest of Britain except on preserved lines. The London and South Western Railway in England were prodigious users of this type.

Barrhill (BR)

Date Built	*c.*1893
G&SW Type or Builder	G&SW Type 7
No. of Levers	18
Way of Working	ETT
Current Status	Active
Listed Scottish Heritage (Y/N)	N

Barrhill signal box layout goes back to the days when the signals and points might be operated by a 'pointsman' and the tablet apparatus by someone else in the station building. It was as a result of the Abermule disaster in 1921 that the Railway Inspectorate recommended that all signalling apparatus be placed in one building at busy locations. The box was brought here in 1935 after the original box burnt down. It is believed the box originally dated from 1908 and had been at Portpatrick in the southwest corner, where it was superseded in 1934. Barrhill station is in south Ayrshire and is 12 miles 35 chains (20km) from Girvan.

The signal box (Fig. 343) is as small as an eighteen-lever box can get, and the mass of cables to the station building give the game away that not all the signalling equipment is in the box.

Fig. 344 shows the lever frame. There is only one point and facing-point lever combined, blue/black, which, together with the fact it is a cut-down lever, means the loop points are electrically operated. By the same reasoning – and the status indicators on the shelf – the distant signals are colour lights.

The Tyer's tablets that act as authority to proceed and lock and unlock the machines are given to the driver in the pouch and hoop devices hanging up on the far wall. Tyer was a signal pioneer from the same mould as Saxby, and Tyer's equipment can be found all over the world.

Barrhill station building is shown in Fig. 345, with the two tablet machines and associated equipment. Some years after these machines were made – probably in the 1870s – the Royal Navy commissioned a new class of leviathan-type battleship named the Dreadnought class. These machines look as though they used similar construction techniques – somewhat over-engineered by modern standards but built to last, and they have.

The machines, one for each section to Girvan and Glenwhilly, are Tyer's tablet no. 6 types. The device can accommodate several tablets but if there are unequal line movements the tablets have to be manually reconciled with the machines.

Fig. 343 (below)   Barrhill signal box and station building, housing the tablet apparatus, November 2006.

Fig. 344 (right)   Barrhill signal box lever frame, November 2006.

The way of passing a train between Barrhill and Girvan would be as follows:

1. Machines at both ends must be closed off with any tablet withdrawn, replaced in either Barrhill or Girvan to signify there are no trains in the section.

2. The signaller at Barrhill sends a bell code on the brass plunger that is at the bottom of the wooden case on top of the machine frame. In absolute block terms, the code is one beat for call attention, and when that has been acknowledged, four beats for, say, an express passenger train. Any code must be acknowledged at the other end.

3. Barrhill holds down the bell plunger and Girvan presses their plunger and pulls the drawer slide out halfway. This gives Train Approaching on both instruments and ensures Girvan cannot get a tablet out.

4. With Girvan holding down their plunger, Barrhill can now hold down that plunger and, with the other hand, withdraw the drawer slide, which will release a tablet to hand to the driver on the platform at Barrhill, once it has been enclosed in the pouch and hoop assembly we saw in Fig. 344. The indicators change to Train on Line.

5. When the train has arrived at Girvan the tablet is handed to the signaller and inserted in the machine there to unlock the machines at both ends and enable another train to be sent in either direction.

Fig. 345   Barrhill station building and Tyer's tablet apparatus, November 2006.

Not surprisingly there are dedicated phone lines to enable signallers to discuss who is holding what and when. All of this is interlocked with points and signals so that no conflicting moves are possible without a driver going past several signals at danger. All of this would be similarly done with Glenwhilly for a train going there.

The grey box with the yellow button and black label is an override in case of signal failure.

Fig. 346 shows Barrhill station building. While the Tyer's tablet machine has its own bell push, the receiving bell codes are rung out on these absolute block bells. They do not have a tapper key as in normal AB working. Note that the one on the right has no bell cover, just a gong. This gives a different tone to the bell cover instrument so the signaller knows who is calling. The gradient profile diagram is useful so that if a train is divided in section the signaller can figure out what can be done about it.

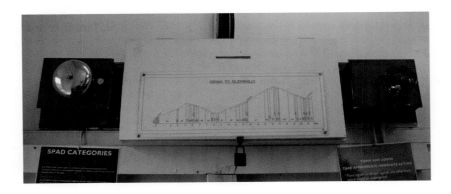

Fig. 346   Barrhill station building and block bells and gradient profile, November 2006.

Fig. 347   *Barrhill station building and Tyer's tablet apparatus with side cover removed, November 2006.*

Fig. 348   *Barrhill station, with the signaller receiving a token and issuing a further token for the next section for the driver of the class 156 DMU, November 2006.*

It is policy on Network Rail now, however, to have vehicles that will automatically come to a stand if disconnected from their train so these diagrams are not as important as they once were. Girvan on the left is almost at sea level so the line mostly climbs.

Barrhill station building appears again in Fig. 347, and here the Tyer's tablet machine is partially undressed. The grey cylinder contains the tablets and the lever operates the drawer slide to access the tablets or lock the machine. The rest of the works are switches and solenoids or electro-mechanical devices that lock the drawer slide and interlock with the machine at the other end of the section. A tablet pouch is hanging from the drawer slide lever. Blue batteries for emergency operation are behind the machine.

In Fig. 348 the signaller exchanges tablets with the driver of the class 156 DMU. SPT is Strathclyde Partnership for Transport. The signaller hangs the received token from the driver around his neck.

Glenwhilly (GW)

Date Built	*c.*1905
G&SW Type or Builder	G&SW Type 7+
No. of Levers	20
Way of Working	ETT
Current Status	Active
Listed Scottish Heritage (Y/N)	N

Fig. 349   *Glenwhilly signal box, November 2006.*

Moving into Dumfries and Galloway, Glenwhilly signal box (Fig. 349) occupies a wild isolated spot that is just a block post, passing loop and siding on the way to Stranraer.

The loop and siding are shown in Fig. 350. The tablet exchange points are well defined, including the moveable steps by the box for higher-up loco cabs. The ground disc guards entry to the siding and there is another with its back to us to let a train out. Its white mini arm is just visible by the trap point. The loop ends just by the second home signal post on the curve in the distance. The view is towards Barrhill. Glenwhilly signal box is 20 miles 70 chains (33.6km) from Girvan.

Fig. 350   Glenwhilly signal box goods loop and tablet platform, November 2006.

The other end of the loop is shown in Fig. 351 with a pair of semaphores to guard it. The box is down an unfenced track and the postman was making a delivery to the box and the house when he came across an extremely large highland cow that was not disposed to move, so he had to do a spot of off-roading to get the delivery done. The view is towards Dunragit. Double-headed boat trains for Stranraer were often held here in steam days as trains coming from Ayr struggled against the gradients. Commonplace performers in steam days were ex-LMS Black Five 4–6–0s and later BR Clan Pacifics.

Wigtownshire Joint Railway (PWJR), over whose metals trains made the final run into Stranraer with a short branch to the Harbour. The PWJR ran to Dumfries from Challoch junction, which closed in 1965 as there was already a line from Kilmarnock through Dumfries to Carlisle. Most stations on the Ayr line also closed in 1965, with Barrhill a notable survivor.

Fig. 351   Glenwhilly end of the loop and re-commencement of the single line to Dunragit, November 2006.

Dunragit (DR)

Date Built	1927
G&SW Type or Builder	LMS Type 12
No. of Levers	32
Way of Working	ETT, KT
Current Status	Active
Listed Scottish Heritage (Y/N)	Y (Category C)

The Glasgow and South Western originally made a junction at Dunragit with the Portpatrick and

Fig. 352 Dunragit signal box, November 2006.

Fig. 353 Dunragit signal box, rear view, November 2006.

From Dunragit to Stranraer the line is worked by key token. Nothing remains of the junction today but it may explain why Dunragit is such a large box for its location and work. It proves that age is not a prerequisite for a listed building – and at Dumfries (*see* later in this chapter) the box is considerably younger still.

In Fig. 352 we can see that Dunragit box has that lookout-type window arrangement at the front that is a common feature on Scottish boxes and is quite distinctive. Dunragit controls the barriers here but the only points are the passing loop. There had been two platforms and two sets of freight sidings here before 1965. The single-line token exchange platform is in position. Dunragit operates one train working to Stranraer when Stranraer Harbour

signal box is switched out. This requires Stranraer Harbour to operate a 'king' lever in the box to cancel the locking that would prevent signals being pulled off for both directions. There is an illustration of this at Lugton on the Carlisle–Glasgow section (*see* later in this chapter).

Fig. 353 shows Dunragit from the side and rear. Thanks to the size of the box it was planned to control part of the line from here when Stranraer Harbour box is done away with. The admin block on the end is almost as large as Barrhill box.

Looking towards Stranraer Harbour, Fig. 354 shows one end of the passing loop. The exchange sidings for Challoch junction were on the right.

Figure 355 shows the other end of the loop, soon to become single track, looking towards Barrhill.

Fig. 354 Dunragit with a view towards Stranraer Harbour and the end of the loop, November 2006.

Fig. 355 Dunragit with a view towards Glenwhilly and the other end of the loop with tablet exchange platform, November 2006.

There is certainly one lattice post signal and what looks like another guarding entry to the loop. Note the modern 'Whistle' board at the loop point.

Stranraer Harbour (SH)

Date Built	1897
G&SW Type or Builder	G&SW Type 3+
No. of Levers	56
Way of Working	KT
Current Status	Dormant
Listed Scottish Heritage (Y/N)	N

Stranraer lies on the banks of Loch Ryan, which provided a sheltered inlet for ferries to Larne in Northern Ireland. It was promoted as the short sea route and for many years a rail sleeper service connected with the ferries. The sleeper trains stopped running in 1990. Various changes of ownership of the ferry companies and a move to Cairnryan on Loch Ryan, a port even closer to Larne and Belfast, saw the port of Stranraer move into decline. There had been extensive goods yards at Stranraer as well as Stranraer Town passenger station. The Town station closed in 1966 but the freight yards ended regular use only in 1993 and were formally closed in 2009. They remain but are overgrown.

The box is now out of use after being only used twice a week for timetabled trains.

Fig. 356 depicts the box heavily muffled up against winter storms with corrugated cladding

Fig. 356   Stranraer Harbour signal box and lattice post platform starter signal, November 2006.

and named Stranraer when some of the signals are plated SH for Stranraer Harbour. The lattice post starter signal for platform 2 on the left cannot see much action as this platform has been out of use for some years. Also the height of the ladder suggests the signal arm has been lowered at some point.

Stranraer Harbour station throat is shown in Fig. 357. The single line from Dunragit comes in past the bracket signal on the left, there are a couple of crossovers and the line splits into two for the platforms on either side. There are two sidings in the middle of the layout, one of which is connected to platform 2 and was originally a loco release crossover. The platform 1 starter signal on the right has a semblance of a finial.

Fig. 357   Stranraer Harbour station platforms and approach track work and signalling, with the view back to Dunragit, November 2006.

Fig. 358 The end of the line at Stranraer Harbour station, November 2006.

Fig. 358 shows Stranraer Harbour station and box looking towards the Loch and the berths for the ferries. Note the use of bullhead rail as a barrier. There used to be roll-on roll-off car ferries here and the *Princess Victoria*, an early type of car ferry, sank on its way from Stranraer on 31 January 1953 in a severe storm. The disaster claimed 134 lives and only forty-two people survived. After that new ships were built and the service improved. At one time there were three double-headed steam trains full of ferry passengers waiting to leave Stranraer.

The buffer stops at Stranraer Harbour station are 54 miles 5 chains (87km) from Girvan.

Carlisle to Glasgow

This route formed the third route to Scotland after the East and West Coast Main Lines. The G&SWR, with the Midland Railway, established a route from St Pancras, Leicester, Nottingham, Sheffield, Leeds and Carlisle through to the route we are to travel. The original terminus was Glasgow St Enoch's station but trains now run from Glasgow Central. St Enoch's architecture was heavily influenced by St Pancras.

We have already seen that coal is shipped from Hunterston in Ayrshire down the G&SW main line to the Settle–Carlisle and thence to coal-fired power

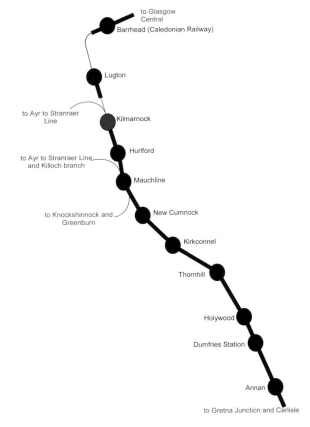

Fig. 359 Carlisle–Glasgow schematic diagram.

stations in England. In addition there are several opencast coal mines in Ayrshire, and that traffic uses the G&SW.

The G&SW influence ends at Lugton, as the succeeding box is of Caledonian Railway origin, one of the few survivors in the Glasgow area. The journey is a continuation of the Settle–Carlisle and therefore runs south to north.

Annan (AN)

Date Built	1876
G&SW Type or Builder	G&SW Type 1
No. of Levers	20
Way of Working	TCB
Current Status	Active
Listed Scottish Heritage (Y/N)	N

The ancestral home of Robert the Bruce is at Annan Castle, and there are many fine buildings in the royal and ancient burgh. The station is also a fine structure and today houses a pub/restaurant which is a local meeting place.

Catching salmon in Solway Firth was a common way to make a living, certainly up until the 1980s, using one of three types of static net moored to the river bed. One local family of salmon fishers recounted the tale of how they exported all their fish to France though the fish exporter's premises were in Grimsby. The fish would be loaded in wooden boxes whose all-up weight when full was 16 stone (just over 100kg). They originally used Eastriggs station until that closed in 1965 then took their fish to Annan, where there was an active goods yard until the 1980s. There were no handling facilities at Annan as the fish was to be put on a passenger train to make its way to Grimsby. The porter's barrow was not quite up to the job and ran off the platform. The signaller was involved in ensuring that any train was checked and stopped until the load was safely back on the platform.

The line from Annan to Gretna Junction had been singled after the electrification of the West Coast Main Line but re-doubled in 2008 when the coal traffic increased. Eastriggs, in common with many other locations in the area, was a base for munitions storage and artillery shell manufacture in World War I.

A train of coal empties rumbles past Annan signal box in Fig. 360 on its way north to Hunterston in Ayrshire. The journey has involved the Settle–Carlisle stretch of the Midland Railway we saw in Chapter 2.

The sidings are the remnants of the goods yard and the trap point is of the two-railed type. Note the modern equivalent of the ground disc indicating that any train proceeding from here, with the aspect given, will end up in the ballast.

Fig. 360   Annan signal box and a train of coal empties heading back to Hunterston in Ayrshire, October 2014.

Fig. 361   Annan station and ultra-bright LED home signal guarding the way to Gretna and Carlisle, October 2014.

Fig. 362   Annan station with old-style colour light signal home signals and single track to Gretna and Carlisle, November 2006.

The fine station at Annan (Fig. 361) is in the Italianate style in local sandstone with canopy and footbridge. Footbridges are an endangered species as they are mostly not disabled access compliant, and some are already listed.

The ultra-bright searchlight LED signal is hard to ignore and a product of modern technology. Light-emitting diodes were only ever useful for panel indicators and the like but the development of ultra-bright versions has meant long life and low power compared to conventional tungsten filament lamps.

A quick rewind to 2006, and Fig. 362 clearly shows the single line to Gretna Junction as well as older-technology colour light signals.

Annan station is 107 miles 19 chains (172.6km) from the former Glasgow Bridge Street station. Note the steam locomotive soot on the overbridge.

Dumfries is a former royal burgh and the county market town that has associations with many population groups from the Romans onwards.

In later times Bonnie Prince Charlie paid a visit to exact tribute but was interrupted and left with not all he came for.

Robert Burns was an Ayrshire man but spent the last years of his life in Dumfries. There are many fine buildings of the local sandstone, the station being one of them.

Dumfries signal box (Fig. 363) proves that a simple architectural style is no barrier to recognition for listing; this style is perhaps best described as 1950s municipal offices. Inside the box there are one-control-switch panels. These panels enable a route to be set up with one switch and all points and

Dumfries Station (DS)

Date Built	1957
G&SW Type or Builder	BR Scottish Region Type 16c
No. of Levers	OCS Panels
Way of Working	TCB, AB
Current Status	Active
Listed Scottish Heritage (Y/N)	Y (Category B)

Fig. 363   Dumfries signal box, November 2006.

signals operate according to the locking, which is usually by relays and track circuits.

Dumfries station boasts a rare survivor from mechanical signalling days in the shape of a banner repeater to display the aspect of the colour light signal at the end of the platform (Fig. 364). These signals had been fairly common where the view of a platform starter signal was obstructed by a station canopy or the curvature of the line. The principle of the banner repeater is still ongoing, except the modern display uses LEDs and fibre-optics. The fine cast iron work in the canopy and has been continued on the footbridge.

In Fig. 365 the former Port bays live underneath a splendid canopy. The Port line was a branch to Stranraer that closed in 1965. The signal referred to in Fig. 364 can just be seen at the end of the platform, and this has a 'feather' or branch for a stub to an oil depot and a former ICI works. The view is looking north towards Kirkconnel and Glasgow.

Looking south towards Annan, Fig. 366 shows another banner repeater on the left-hand platform as well as a modernized ground signal for Leafield Road Yard. This small yard beyond the road overbridge had been used by EWS railways and by the carriage and wagon department.

Dumfries station is 91 miles 63 chains (147.7km) from the former Glasgow Bridge Street station.

Fig. 364 Dumfries station and banner repeater signal, November 2006.

Fig. 365 Dumfries station with the former Port line bays, which are now a car park, looking towards Glasgow, November 2006.

Fig. 366 Dumfries station with another banner repeater on the left-hand platform, looking towards Annan, November 2006.

Holywood (HW)

Date Built	18??
G&SW Type or Builder	G&SW Type 7+
No. of Levers	23
Way of Working	AB
Current Status	Active
Listed Scottish Heritage (Y/N)	N

Fig. 367   Holywood signal box and gates, November 2006.

The mists of time have descended over the records of when this box was built (Fig. 367). The station opened in 1849 and closed in 1949 but the box is likely to be of the 1870s. There are only a handful of boxes left in Britain that still use a gate wheel from the box to open and close the gates, although there are examples on the preserved railways. The operation of the main road gates and side wicket gates is interlocked with the semaphore signals. There are no points here. There are massive iron supports that will extend some way beneath the surface to support the weight, as the gates act as a big lever. Note that the gates are not actually locked in position.

Fig. 368 shows the view towards Dumfries, with the former Holywood station platform on the left. The oil lamp on the gate is an early relic but was not lit at the time of the survey. Some of the mechanical linkages that operate the gates from the box can be seen behind the gates.

The view towards Kirkconnel is shown in Fig. 369. The oil lamp presents a red aspect to the road when the gates are closed.

Holywood signal box is 88 miles 31 chains (142.2km) from the former Glasgow Bridge Street station.

Thornhill (TH)

Date Built	1943
G&SW Type or Builder	LMS Type 13c
No. of Levers	30
Way of Working	AB
Current Status	Active
Listed Scottish Heritage (Y/N)	N

Fig. 368   Holywood signal box gates and the line to Dumfries, October 2014.

Fig. 369   Holywood signal box gates and oil lamp and the line to Glasgow, October 2014.

The Duke of Buccleuch and Queensberry decreed that this bit of the G&SWR should not be visible from his ancestral home at Drumlanrig Castle nearby. The line made a detour from the Nith valley to comply and the station is over a mile from the town and somewhat inconvenient for it. It closed in 1965.

The LMS built many air raid precautions (ARP) boxes during World War II. Many came about as a result of changes to track layouts needed for increased facilities, and some were replacements for bomb damage. Fig. 370 shows just such a box at Thornhill.

Fig. 371 shows the view north towards Glasgow and the station platforms in position, complete with station house, now in private hands. The trailing crossover gives access to the up goods loop, where the up direction is towards Carlisle. The lattice post signal is for the main line south and the smaller signal to enter the goods loop behind the camera. The former goods yard is to the left and the weigh-bridge is still used as an office by the business that currently occupies the site.

Looking back the other way towards Dumfries, the up goods loop entry can be seen in Fig. 372. There is often a catch point near the entry to the loop. This is to derail any runaway vehicle from fouling the main line, and they are usually spring loaded. Perhaps the gradient profile here means that catch points are not required. Catch points are quite different from trap points, which are lever operated.

Fig. 370   Thornhill signal box, October 2014.

Fig. 371   Thornhill station platforms and station building and the view towards Glasgow, November 2006.

Fig. 372   Thornhill signal box and goods loops and the view towards Dumfries, November 2006.

Kirkconnel (KC)

Date Built	*c.*1911
G&SW Type or Builder	G&SW Type 7+
No. of Levers	42
Way of Working	AB
Current Status	Active
Listed Scottish Heritage (Y/N)	N

Fig. 373   Kirkconnel signal box, October 2014.

The village was known mostly as a farming community but there was also a coal mine right behind the signal box. Earlier pictures show a massive coal tip parallel with the running line, but Fig. 373 shows no evidence of this earlier coal mining activity. The box is different in that it was extended when modernized in 2000 by the addition of the admin block on the end by the steps.

The massive coal tip was behind the home signal on the left of Fig. 374. The station is beyond that, with only the footbridge surviving out of the original buildings. Kirkconnel has a trailing crossover and a couple of engineer's sidings from the original layout. Note the lonesome ground signal on the far right of the picture. To the right of the sidings was an elevated loading dock whose origins remain. There is a manual point lever for the outermost siding.

Fig. 375 is looking back from the station platform. Access to the sidings and goods yard was signalled by the doll or subsidiary arm of the bracket signal in the foreground, now unarmed. It seems hardly credible that there was a massive coal tip on the right of the picture. The view is towards Glasgow. The station is 62 miles 31 chains (100.4km) from the former Glasgow Bridge Street station and is the last stop in Dumfries and Galloway before entering Ayrshire.

Fig. 374   Kirkconnel station and sidings towards Dumfries, October 2014.

New Cumnock (NC)

Date Built	1909
G&SW Type or Builder	G&SW Type 7+
No. of Levers	40
Way of Working	AB
Current Status	Active
Listed Scottish Heritage (Y/N)	N

Fig. 375   *The view from Kirkconnel station platform towards Glasgow, October 2014.*

New Cumnock is associated with William Wallace, whose exploits were dramatized in the Academy award-winning film *Braveheart*. Robert the Bruce sought refuge in the town and Robert Burns was a frequent visitor.

More recently the town was associated with coal mining, being part of the Ayrshire coalfield, though the last opencast mine closed in May 2013. In 1950 a mining disaster at nearby Knockshinnoch Castle Colliery killed thirteen people.

The signal box (Fig. 376) has been heavily modernized and modified to contain a panel to work the Knockshinnoch and Greenburn branches that lead to collieries but its origins are unmistakeable.

Fig. 377 shows the layout looking towards Kirkconnel. Beyond the second overbridge is a co-acting home signal whose lattice post can just be seen rising above the bridge parapet. This signal has two arms, one lower and one upper. The upper gives sighting some distance away and the lower, as in this case, nearer to the train.

Fig. 378 shows New Cumnock station looking towards Mauchline and Glasgow. The loop that goes around behind the platform gives access to a former colliery siding and there is still some coal activity there. Note that there is a very short

Fig. 376   *New Cumnock signal box, October 2014.*

Fig. 377   *New Cumnock station and co-acting signal in the distance, November 2006.*

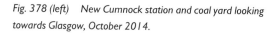

Fig. 378 (left)   New Cumnock station and coal yard looking towards Glasgow, October 2014.

Fig. 379 (centre)   New Cumnock station. A Colas Rail class 56 labours up the gradient with a Network Rail ballast train, assisted in the rear by a Colas Rail class 66, October 2014.

Fig. 380 (below)   New Cumnock station and a double-decker lattice post ground disc signal, October 2014.

headshunt or trap point with buffer stops and trailing crossover.

The reason for the signals being in the off position has arrived in Fig. 379 – a Colas Rail class 56 with a Network Rail ballast train that is so heavy it needs a Colas Rail class 66 to push as well. The inclination of the wagons shows how steep the gradient becomes just here. The train has breasted Polquap summit, at 616ft (188m), which is about 2 miles (3km) back down the line.

Finally at New Cumnock, Fig. 380 shows another rare signal. This double elevated ground disc on a lattice post guards the exit from the goods loop we saw in Fig. 378.

New Cumnock station is 54 miles 72 chains (88.4km) from the former Glasgow Bridge Street station.

Mauchline (MM)

Date Built	1909
G&SW Type or Builder	G&SW Type 1+
No. of Levers	35
Way of Working	AB
Current Status	Active
Listed Scottish Heritage (Y/N)	N

Mauchline village was a haunt of Robert Burns and a place where curling stones are manufactured from solid granite. It is also famous for Mauchline ware, which is wooden carved objects that were transfer printed with designs of resorts or tartans. They were produced as souvenirs for visitors on holiday and have become highly prized by collectors. The last factory burnt down in 1933 and production then ceased.

Mauchline is also a junction for the line to Newton-on-Ayr and Ayr Harbour.

The line is single track and works no signaller key token. This means that after a token has been issued at Mauchline, the train driver operates the ancillary token instrument down the line, which is controlled and locked by the instrument at Mauchline. Mauchline signal box is shown in Fig. 381. The pair of tracks right in front of the box are the double-track main line from Kilmarnock on the left and Carlisle on the right. The other two tracks are basically a loop leading to a single-track branch line on the left; the loop extends for less than half a mile (1km).

Looking towards Carlisle now, Fig. 382 shows the site of the station that was closed in 1965. The trailing crossover appears to have rail clamp point locks on the two points. The taller post is the home signal for the Kilmarnock direction and the shorter is for the Newton-on-Ayr branch. The smaller signal is actually a bracket that may have had another post and arm on in the past. There appear to be two operating bellcranks lower down the main post.

There are three sidings, which are connected to the up side of the loop, which is towards Newton-on-Ayr – the buffer stops of one of them are just visible on the right.

Fig. 381   Mauchline signal box, December 2014.

The camera turns the other way in Fig. 383. The short signal is the home signal that protects the main line from trains coming off the branch, which is the down direction. Beyond the signal is a walkway and token-handover elevated platforms: the one on the left is to issue the token and the one on the right to retrieve it. The main line to Kilmarnock curves around to the right.

Fig. 384 shows the Newton-on-Ayr branch setting off on its journey; the smaller home signal

Fig. 382   Mauchline station site and the Carlisle direction, December 2014.

Fig. 383   Mauchline with main line in front of the signal box and branch loop to the left and the Glasgow direction, December 2014.

Fig. 384   Mauchline with the branch loop and the taller signal guarding the main line towards Glasgow, December 2014.

Fig. 385   Mauchline with the branch loop and the fan of three sidings with headshunt. The branch is worked NSKT to Newton-on-Ayr, hence the token platform, December 2014.

on the left is the precursor to the start of the single-line section. The main line to Kilmarnock is out of sight on the right behind the growth and guarded by the taller home signal on the right. The lead-off point for the three sidings is in the foreground. The small white signal arm on the ground disc signal that proves it has worked shows up well here.

Fig. 385 shows the branch loop with its three sidings; the one on the far left is termed 'engineer's siding' on TrackMaps. The lead in from the up part of the Newton-on-Ayr branch is on the left and forms a crossover with the headshunt on the extreme right of the picture. All the track looks well used, even the headshunt. There is a coal washery and blending plant at Killoch, where once there had been a colliery.

Mauchline signal box is 43 miles 10 chains (69.4km) from the former Glasgow Bridge Street station.

Hurlford (H)

Date Built	1920s
G&SW Type or Builder	LMS Type 12
No. of Levers	20
Way of Working	AB
Current Status	Closed
Listed Scottish Heritage (Y/N)	N

Fig. 386   Hurlford signal box, October 2014.

Hurlford developed rapidly in the nineteenth century after the discovery nearby of coal, ironstone and fireclay. All these industries had ceased by the 1970s. The station closed some years ago but there are moves by local authorities for a halt to be established. The production of Scotch whisky had its own railway depot complete with locomotive shed a short way from the box. This was later a warehouse but now even this work has ceased.

Hurlford is on the outskirts of Kilmarnock and this was the locomotive works for the G&SWR. The works of Andrew Barclay, established in 1840, are an astonishing survivor of locomotive manufacturing, as the passing years have seen the demise of nearly all of Britain's capacity in that regard. The company trades as Wabtec Rail Scotland.

After many years of only being manned sporadically the box is now closed and boarded up.

Hurlford signal box is 35 miles 50 chains (57.3km) from the former Glasgow Bridge Street station.

Lugton (LU)

Date Built	1929
G&SW Type or Builder	LMS Type 12+
No. of Levers	35
Way of Working	TB
Current Status	Active
Listed Scottish Heritage (Y/N)	N

North of Kilmarnock we come onto the single lines that run to Barrhead, which is former Caledonian Railway territory. From there the outer suburban system runs to Glasgow.

Lugton grew as a result of the crossing of two turnpike roads in the early nineteenth century. Later two railways had stations here but there are no stations now although there is local agitation to open a halt. The line is a long passing loop that goes into a single line at each end, which is worked tokenless block in both directions. There are plans to reinstate double track hereabouts and this would mean the end of TB working here. There are the remnants of sidings here, and there was a

Fig. 387   Lugton signal box, October 2014.

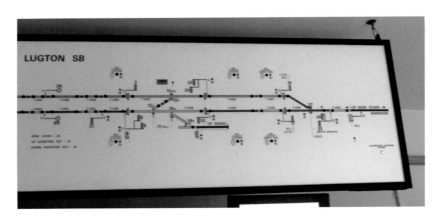

Fig. 388   Lugton signal box interior and diagram, October 2014.

branch line to a Royal Naval Armaments depot, later termed Defence Munitions, at Beith. The last train ran in 1996 but the track is still in position.

Lugton signal box, shown in Fig. 387, is quite an imposing structure, with the side lookout window type known in railway circles as a 'ducket'. This term is usually applied to the older-style brake van or passenger coach brake where a side window is grafted onto the side of the vehicle, allowing a guard to view up and down the line from the vehicle without having to open a window and lean out.

Part of the track diagram is shown in Fig. 388. The single line to Barrhead is on the right and both lines of the loop are bi-directionally signalled. For example, signals 17 and 19 would both signal a train down towards Glasgow but are mutually exclusive operationally and in locking terms.

The trailing crossover in front of the box is not signalled with subsidiary arms and passenger trains can use it; this is further reinforced by the fact that the crossover has a facing-point lock, lever 13. Lever 11 is not only the facing-point lock for the other point in the crossover but for the siding

Fig. 389   Lugton signal box interior and block shelf with Scottish tokenless block instrument with the two green lights, October 2014.

point as well. This would mean that it would be impossible to change the siding point while the crossover was reversed. This interlock feature would be integrated into the mechanical locking of the frame.

The siding, on the other hand, just has a ground disc, and note how the trap point is operated by the same lever – 14 – as the siding point, just as if it were a crossover, which in a sense it is. Each change of colour denotes a different track circuit, which lights up if occupied by a train.

Part of the lever frame and block shelf can be seen in Fig. 389. The two monitors on the shelf are for the signaller to observe a train leaving the section at either end so that the train can be observed complete with tail lamp. This is necessary to ensure that a train has not divided in the section. In the railways of the past, with loose-coupled goods trains, a broken coupling was not uncommon, and the reason that a brake van was always marshalled at the rear of a train was that the guard could be relied upon to bring that part of a divided train to a stand. In absolute block territory the signaller would bell 2 pause 1 for Train out of Section to the next box where the train was headed.

The two blue boxes are Scottish tokenless block instruments, one for Barrhead and one for Kilmarnock. Although quite different in hardware terms, they operate on the same principle as the TB we have already seen at Park South and Barrow on the Furness Railway in Chapter 4. Also noteworthy are the signal status indicators built into the edge of the block shelf. This and the instruments were built by BR Scottish Region and look neater and more professional than some other installations.

Fig. 390 shows the frame itself, with lever 20 as a brown and white hybrid. This box is equipped with a switch, which means it can be switched out of circuit and bypassed. This happens at night here. On single lines the interlocking would prevent a train being signalled in both directions at the same time. When a box is switched out all signals must be off so that any driver can pass that box's section signals in either direction.

Lever 20 is the 'king lever' that negates all the conflicting signalling locking to enable the box to be switched out. It has to be pulled to the centre point as marked on the frame. Note the ivorine plates describing what each lever does at the rear of the frame.

Fig. 390   Lugton signal box interior and lever frame with brass shunt key inserted on the far right, October 2014.

Fig. 391   Lugton with a train due from Kilmarnock in the Carlisle direction, October 2014.

On the far right-hand side of the frame is a black box attached to the frame from which protrudes a brass key; this is right next to the unused lever 35. This is a shunt key, which allows a train to intrude into the next section without being signalled as a dispatched train. Clearly the operation of the shunt key blocks any subsequent attempt to dispatch a train into the occupied section. There are special bell codes to inform signallers at the other boxes that a shunt key is in use and that its use has terminated. This box is equipped with a shunt key for both ends of the layout.

In Fig. 391 a train is expected from Kilmarnock, which is the normal up direction on this line.

Note the bracket signal for the crossover outside the box on the other track and the two speed-restriction signs confirming possible bi-directional working.

Looking towards Barrhead and Glasgow and the normal down direction in Fig. 392, a train is being signalled from there. The siding opposite the box used to belong to Hydro Agriculture but has been 'plain lined', although the actual siding track and trap point off it are still in situ. The signals 17 and 19 referred to in Fig. 388 are about 30 chains or less than half a mile (600m) from here.

Mileages change north of Kilmarnock, and Lugton signal box is 13 miles 50 chains (21.9km) from the former Gorbals Junction.

From here to Glasgow the line was GSWR and Caledonian Railway joint. The next box is Barrhead, which is the former CR and consequently will be covered in LMS Volume 2.

Fig. 392   Lugton with a train due from Barrhead in the Glasgow direction, October 2014.

CHAPTER 6

North Staffordshire Railway

The North Staffordshire Railway was to modernize the Staffordshire Potteries, who had originally imported clay and coal for the manufacture of pottery and exported the finished products along the Trent and Mersey Canal in the eighteenth century. By 1760 Josiah Wedgwood had industrialized and perfected the manufacture of porcelain and pottery wares.

The North Staffordshire Railway (NSR) centred on Stoke-on-Trent but had lines radiating out to Cheshire, Shropshire and Derbyshire as well as Staffordshire.

The railway only had a route mileage of 221 miles (356km) and so would seem to have been an ideal candidate for amalgamation with one of the larger companies that surrounded it. The NSR resisted all overtures, however, and in due course became a constituent of the LMS in 1923. The railway is nicknamed 'The Knotty' from the pretzel-shaped knot that is the symbol of Staffordshire. There is a legend that three felons were due to be hung in Stafford gaol in medieval times and to ensure that all three were dispatched simultaneously, the hangman devised the knot depicted in the county badge. However, the knot is also seen elsewhere at an earlier period.

There are street names in the area which have 'Old Knotty', meaning the NSR, in the title.

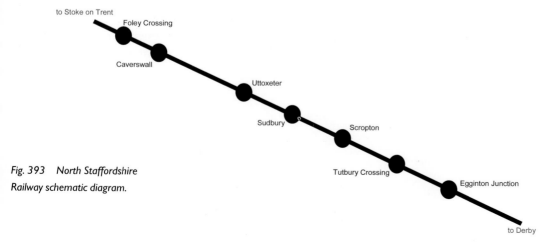

Fig. 393 North Staffordshire Railway schematic diagram.

Fig. 394   Foley Crossing signal box, October 2004.

Stoke-on-Trent to Derby

Apart from the Churnet Valley preserved railway, which was one of the earliest parts of the NSR, the sole surviving line of the NSR with mechanical signalling is the line from Stoke-on-Trent to Derby. The journey begins in the 'Potteries' area of Stoke-on-Trent.

Foley Crossing (FY)

Date Built	1889
NSR Type or Builder	North Staffs 2+
No. of Levers	37
Way of Working	TCB, AB
Current Status	Active
Listed (Y/N)	N

Foley Crossing is just out of Longton station in Stoke-on-Trent and is so named after the James Kent pottery, who manufactured a range of porcelain products named 'Old Foley'. Their works was just over the tracks from the box and many workers used the crossing to get to the works. The area was surrounded by potteries and some of the unusual coal-fired bottle kilns are still in evidence today.

Fig. 394 shows Foley Crossing signal box in 2004 in largely unmodernized state. The frames in many of the NSR boxes were manufactured by Mackenzie and Holland, as they did not have their own signal works. Note that there is a surviving bottle kiln in the distance. This box works TCB to Stoke power box and AB to Caverswall towards Derby.

Foley Crossing signal box is seen from the other side of the tracks in Fig. 395. Manually operated wooden gates are quite rare but turnstiles to stop the thronging workforce spilling onto the track were unusual.

Fig. 396 is the view looking towards Longton station with a modernized banner repeater signal giving advance warning about the aspect ahead around the curve. They use a combination of fibre-optics and LEDs. Fibre-optics enable light to be shone down a flexible glass pipe virtually without loss of brilliance. The platform of what looks like a disused works halt is just past the signal, while a track-circuited semaphore signal guards the crossing.

Looking the other way towards Stoke-on-Trent, Fig. 397 shows a similar arrangement with regard to both signal and bottle kiln. The large sign with 'I' on it is a reference to Interim Voice Radio System

Fig. 395   Foley Crossing signal box with gates, cobbles and turnstile, October 2004.

Fig. 396   Foley Crossing signal box looking towards Longton, November 2014.

Fig. 397   Foley Crossing signal box looking towards Derby, November 2014.

(IVRS), which is the way drivers and signallers communicate via a GSM digital mobile phone-type system. This is used in areas where axle counter train detection has replaced conventional track circuits. Axle counters count the number of axles entering a section and then count the same number out. If there is a discrepancy, signals turn to red and alarms sound as it indicates a train has become divided in the section. The 'I' indicates commencement of IVRS and the same board with a red line through it, the termination.

Foley Crossing signal box is 1 mile 56 chains (2.7km) from Wedgwood Junction, which is close to Stoke-on-Trent station.

Caverswall (CL)

Date Built	1942
NSR Type or Builder	LMS Type 11c
No. of Levers	35
Way of Working	AB
Current Status	Active
Listed (Y/N)	N

Caverswall Castle is a local stately home that has been home to Lord Wedgwood, a group of Benedictine nuns, the Chief Constable of Staffordshire Police and the infamous Victorian fraudster known as the Tichborne Claimant – but not all at the same time.

Caverswall signal box (Fig. 398) is just on the outskirts of Stoke-on-Trent and as well as a crossing has both up and down goods loops. In this case down is towards Stoke-on-Trent and up is towards Derby. The house in the background of the picture is the former crossing keeper's house and was built by the same architect who built Stoke-on-Trent station for the NSR in the Dutch style. The railway station at Stone has similarities and is Grade II listed. The couple who own it have restored many of the original NSR features, including the bathroom tiles.

Fig. 398   Caverswall signal box and crossing house in the Dutch style, November 2014.

Fig. 399   Caverswall looking towards Stoke-on-Trent, November 2014.

Fig. 400   Caverswall looking towards Derby with goods loops and facing-point lock, November 2014.

Fig. 399 shows Caverswall signal box crossing and the view towards Foley Crossing and Stoke-on-Trent. The ground discs signal reversing moves over the trailing crossover and the double-decker on the left also signals a train to reverse into the up goods loop. The home signal is Caverswall 24.

Caverswall signal box crossing and the goods loops are shown in Fig. 400. The facing point to enter the up loop on the right has its lock bar bolt clearly visible on the point stretcher bar between the two point blades. The facing-point lock bolt locates into notches in the stretcher bar to stop the point from moving underneath the train. The facing-point lock bolt must be withdrawn before the point can be changed over.

On the up line a little further on is the Foxfield Railway, which is a standard gauge industrial preserved railway based on the former Foxfield colliery.

Caverswall signal box is 4 miles 20 chains (6.8km) from Wedgwood Junction.

Uttoxeter (UR)

Date Built	1981
NSR Type or Builder	BR London Midland Region Type 15c
No. of Levers	40
Way of Working	AB
Current Status	Active
Listed (Y/N)	N

Nearby Rocester is the home of JCB, that world-class example of superb British engineering, and at the end of this line at Derby is the home of Rolls Royce aero engines, another in the same bracket.

Uttoxeter signal box was the last mechanical signal box installed on Network Rail. Until the 1960s Uttoxeter had been a junction for the line to Leek and Macclesfield in Cheshire with a loco depot. It is much reduced in size and status but retains a modernized passenger station, down goods loop and engineer's siding.

The box looks quite sprightly in Fig. 401, as it should do at less than thirty-five years old. As well as the crossing it stands near, it has to supervise two more by CCTV.

Fig. 401   Uttoxeter signal box, November 2014.

Fig. 402   Uttoxeter signal box with the view towards Derby and the engineer's siding, November 2014.

Looking towards Derby in Fig. 402, the engineer's siding is a repository for permanent way materials and has been cut back from three sidings to one. The buffer stops here look well camouflaged whereas most of them, not surprisingly, are bright yellow or red. The bracket signal subsidiary arm allows entry into the down goods loop behind the camera; the other subsidiary arm over the tracks is, unusually, for reversing over the crossover, which is track circuited, also behind the camera. Note the trailing point in the foreground has none of the facing-point lock equipment that we saw at Caverswall up goods loop.

Fig. 403 is the view towards Caverswall from the engineer's yard, and the trailing crossover and down goods loop can be seen past the box. The crossing has been restricted to pedestrians only. The yard on the right used to store JCB machines.

Fig. 403   Uttoxeter signal box with the view towards Caverswall and the engineer's siding and down goods loop past the box, November 2014.

Fig. 404   Uttoxeter at Hockley Crossing by the down goods loop with a class 153 DMU sprinting towards Derby, November 2014.

Fig. 405   Uttoxeter lattice post signal, October 2005.

A class 153 DMU hurries along past Hockley Crossing by the end of the down goods loop towards the box and Derby in Fig. 404.

The up section from Caverswall to Uttoxeter is quite long at nearly 12 miles (19km) and is divided up by an intermediate block section (IBS). This tends to indicate an increased frequency of freight trains on the route in recent years.

Going back about ten years, the first survey revealed the lattice post signal in Fig. 405. It is known that the NSR had lattice post signals so this signal could be about eighty years old at the time of the photograph in 2005, or it is possible it was in store and erected by the LMS subsequently.

Uttoxeter signal box is 16 miles (26km) from Wedgwood Junction.

Sudbury (SY)

Date Built	1885
NSR Type or Builder	North Staffs 1
No. of Levers	25
Way of Working	AB
Current Status	Active
Listed (Y/N)	Y

Fig. 406   Sudbury signal box and garden, November 2014.

Fig. 407   Sudbury signal box rear and side view, October 2005.

We now leave Staffordshire behind and move into Derbyshire.

Sudbury Hall is a fine seventeenth-century mansion which was the ancestral home of the Vernon family but now belongs to the National Trust. It also houses a residence where people must stay as guests of Her Majesty.

Sudbury signal box is on the busy A515 road and has seemingly been retained for that reason. There are no points and just a couple of colour light signals that can be seen from the crossing. The box looks completely original in Fig. 406 and must have been an obvious candidate for listing. There is no tacked-on admin block, just a blue Portaloo.

The signal box has been embellished by its occupants over the years and some of that is retained. Note the Staffordshire county emblem of the knot and reference to the NSR together with the box build date. Even in the autumn there are pots and hanging baskets to signify cultivation as well as the small garden. The lamp hut is an extraordinary survivor with its impossibly complicated windows for a corrugated iron structure. Note also the railway oil lamp outside. The two battens on the wall nearest the crossing used to hold an advertising poster from the Great Northern Railway for a trip to Skegness. The poster is well known and declares

'Skegness is so bracing', by the artist John Hassall; the original is in the Victoria and Albert Museum. Skegness holiday trains from Stoke passed this box.

Looking at Sudbury signal box from the side and rear (Fig. 407), the aforementioned poster can just be seen. It would seem the house next door was built after the box, as the lookout window for the road seems to be obstructed by it.

Sudbury signal box is 20 miles 67 chains (33.5km) from Wedgwood Junction.

Scropton

Date Built	*c.*1884
NSR Type or Builder	North Staffs 2
No. of Levers	22
Way of Working	AB
Current Status	Active
Listed (Y/N)	N

Scropton is a delightful village on a minor road and the box is on a road off the minor road. Whereas Sudbury had no mechanical devices, Scropton is virtually all mechanical.

Scropton is another box from the Mackenzie and Holland stable and many typical attributes are present and correct (Fig. 408). The box has

Fig. 408   Scropton (Crossing) signal box, November 2014.

Fig. 409   Scropton signal box with the view towards Stoke-on-Trent, November 2014.

Fig. 410   Scropton signal box with the view towards Derby as class 153 rattles over the trailing crossover, November 2014.

Fig. 411   Scropton signal box interior with diagram and absolute block instruments, November 2014.

'Crossing' appended to its name on the front but is known as Scropton.

In the foreground an over-zealous road mender has covered the mechanical linkages to the wicket gates in tarmac so they no longer work; perhaps an inverted steel trough would have done the job. The legend on the gate post reads 'NSR Co. 1884 LMS 1923'.

Fig. 409 shows the view towards Stoke-on-Trent, with the trailing crossover prominent. Not so prominent are the welded rail joins just after the point on the down side towards Stoke and the angled cranks of the point rodding on the left. By varying the lengths and angle of the cranks it is possible to vary the throw of the point lever. This can either extend or reduce the distance that the point rodding, and hence the point tie-bar, moves. In addition there is often a turnbuckle on the rod ends, which allows for smaller adjustments. A turnbuckle is a nut on the rod which is static, but a screw-threaded rod extension is wound in and out to vary the distance travelled. There is only one rod for a trailing crossover.

The class 153 in Fig. 410 is heading for Derby, past another trailing crossover. When the class 153 reaches the end of Scropton's section the signaller will give 2 pause 1 on the block bell to signify Train out of Section to Tutbury, the next box along. This can only be given if the tail lights are observed,

confirming the train is complete, as we can see they are in this case. Where the tail lights are not visible but the train is complete, for example round a curve, a CCTV camera is provided so the signaller can still confirm the train's completeness and give Train out of Section. The modernized version is a system of axle counters, which does away with this requirement.

Inside the box in Fig. 411 we can see the two BR 'domino' absolute block instruments that control movements, together with the signalling diagram. The instruments tend to be at the end of the shelf in the direction they are communicating with, which ties up with the diagram.

Scropton–Sudbury – Up and Down Lines

On the left the Sudbury instrument is showing Train on Line on the down part of the instrument, which is on top in this case. The acceptance part of the line for Scropton – which is the up for Sudbury – is next to the acceptance lever or commutator.

This means that a train has been sent to Sudbury from Scropton on the down and is still in Scropton's section. At this point the Scropton signaller gives Sudbury the special bell code of 1 pause 2 pause 1 beat on the Sudbury instrument. This means Train Approaching and is given because the section is quite short, at less than two miles (3km). This is a warning that the train will be at Sudbury very quickly.

On the lower part of Sudbury's instrument, the up line, Scropton has set Line Clear for a train coming from Sudbury but it is not at Scropton yet.

Scropton–Tutbury – Up and Down Lines

On the Tutbury instrument, the signaller there has accepted the train for Derby on the up, which is the one just being received by Scropton from Sudbury.

There is no train movement from Tutbury to Scropton on the down line at present.

On the diagram only one crossover is depicted but neither of them is in operation and the point lever has a collar on it. The diagram also shows only one track circuit on the layout, coloured yellow – no. 2601.

The Mackenzie and Holland lever frame dominates Fig. 412. A good many of the levers have collars on them, as they are temporarily out of use. This has been going on for some months now. As the box is due to go in 2017 there will be reluctance to get it all working properly only to close it. There are tales of British Railways doing exactly that and then closing something down because it was claimed to cost a lot to maintain.

At each end of the layout is a yellow distant signal lever (lever 1), and the up signal on the left is 1,400yd from the home signal, lever 2, which makes it a mile from the box. Steel wires expand with hot weather and the L-shaped black lever at the back of the frame and behind lever 21 (nearest the camera) is the signal wire adjuster handle. There is more than one adjuster but only one handle in the box.

The board with the ivorine plates with the signal function labels on it, behind the frame, also has the inscription 'MACKENZIE AND HOLLAND SIGNAL ENGINEERS WORCESTER' on it.

The black lever and red levers associated with the crossover on the diagram are out of use, with collars on them.

The two circular instruments at each end of the block shelf are signal status indicators for the two distant signals. They have a miniature signal arm

Fig. 412   Scropton signal box interior with the lever frame and block shelf, November 2014.

Fig. 413 Scropton signal box interior with lever frame detail, November 2014.

that moves with the signal. If the power to the transmitter fails, it reads 'Wrong'.

The other circular instrument at the nearest end to the camera and inboard of the signal instrument is an indicator for the track circuit. The tall black box at the far end of the shelf is a 'Lamp Out' indicator box, with a buzzer for the distant signals that are not in view from the box.

Also of note is the worn and smooth state of the wooden plank across the end of the frame. This has been used by generations of signallers to gain purchase with a foot to help swing the levers over.

Fig. 413 shows part of the Mackenzie and Holland lever frame complete with what looks like an NSR badge. The three flags kept in reserve in case all else fails are stacked against the wall. The three brown levers are for the wicket gates – levers 20 and 21, which no longer operate, and the main gate locks, lever 22. The gates are hand operated or in technical parlance 'handraulic', but the lock must first be released. The gate locks also have electrical heaters on them as they can freeze up in winter.

Note how some signal levers can be pulled part way across the frame by the various notches in the frame as partial compensation for the ambient temperature. The signal adjuster for the down distant is behind the frame, with its toothed gear wheel that actually tightens/slackens the signal wire.

Also the down distant, lever 19, must have levers 17 and 18 pulled first. This piece of information is painted on the 19 lever. The white band on the red lever home signal no. 17 indicates that it is electrically locked by another function rather than just mechanically locked in the frame, as just described, by the distant signal.

Scropton signal box is 22 miles 53 chains (36.5km) from Wedgwood Junction.

Tutbury Crossing

Date Built	c.1872
NSR Type or Builder	Mackenzie and Holland Type 1
No. of Levers	9
Way of Working	AB
Current Status	Active
Listed (Y/N)	N

Tutbury Castle imprisoned Mary Queen of Scots for a few short spells in the sixteenth century. Tutbury also manufactured fine-quality crystal but the factory moved to newer premises in 2005.

Tutbury Crossing is one of the oldest signal boxes (Fig. 414) on Network Rail and survives as a crossing place and block post. There are no points here any more. The goods shed is still there but now a Buildbase builder's merchant depot. The main road divides the station platforms. The station was closed in the 1960s but reopened in 1989. The

Fig. 414 (right)   Tutbury Crossing signal box, November 2014.

Fig. 415 (centre)   Tutbury Crossing and the adjacent platform across the road looking towards Stoke-on-Trent, November 2014.

London Midland maroon sign survived the 1960s closure.

Fig. 415 shows Tutbury and Hatton station, looking across the road to the down platform towards Stoke. The Buildbase goods shed is behind the platform on the far left.

Fig. 416 is looking towards Derby. The renewed signal is to replace a bracket signal canted over the track.

Egginton Junction (EN)

Date Built	1877
NSR Type or Builder	North Staffs Type 1
No. of Levers	14
Way of Working	AB, TCB
Current Status	Active
Listed (Y/N)	N

Egginton Junction formerly was a junction station that saw the Great Northern Railway run into the NSR. The Great Northern ran from here to Derby

Fig. 416   Tutbury Crossing looking towards Derby, November 2014.

Fig. 417   Egginton Junction signal box, November 2014.

Fig. 418   Egginton Junction looking towards Stoke-on-Trent and the former MoD sidings on the right, complete with loading gauge, November 2014.

Fig. 419   Looking towards Derby and the road crossing that Egginton Junction signal box supervises, November 2014.

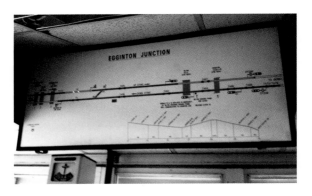

Friargate station, which has long since been closed and demolished.

There were sidings to a Ministry of Defence depot; they are still in position but not connected to the main line any longer.

The signal box (Fig. 417) is of prodigious height for the NSR and would appear to be this high for sighting purposes.

Fig. 418 is looking towards Stoke, and we can see the trailing crossover that forms the only points surviving on the layout. The frame of the loading gauge for the MoD sidings is just on the right of the home signal. Note how the signals have both had their arms lowered on the post and the lamps left up the posts.

Looking towards Derby, Fig. 419 shows the crossing with manually operated gates that are released from the signal box. The crossing keeper's Portakabin can be seen on the right-hand side of the road opposite the original palatial example. The original station buildings of the junction station are now in private hands and are to the left behind the hedge.

Fig. 420   Egginton Junction signal box diagram with a train occupying a track circuit, November 2014.

Fig. 421   Egginton Junction signal box lever frame and block shelf. Note there is only one absolute block instrument, November 2014.

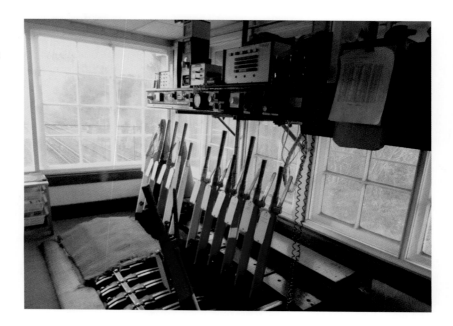

Inside Egginton Junction signal box, the diagram in Fig. 420 has Train in Section lit up heading for Derby on the right of the diagram.

Egginton Junction signal box frame is shown in Fig. 421. There are only fourteen levers, though the frame had forty-seven when originally installed. Lever 14 in the foreground is actually blue and brown and it is the release for the locks for the gates we saw in Fig. 419. In view of the distance, the locking is purely electrical. There is only one domino block instrument as the box works track circuit block to Derby. There is a block bell for communication with Derby in an emergency and this is tested every morning. The red hand wheel near the floor on the right hand side is a signal wire adjuster.

Fig. 422 shows the signal box lever frame and a true NSR relic with a lever collar in position.

The line continues for another 2 miles (3km) before the junction with the former Midland Railway and the run into Derby Midland station.

If you have enjoyed the journeys so far, the LMS story continues in Volume 2 with the London and North Western, Caledonian and Highland Railways.

Fig. 422   Egginton Junction signal box lever frame and an original North Staffordshire lever collar, November 2014.

Useful Resources

Books and Written Works

Allan, I., *British Railways Pre-Grouping Atlas and Gazetteer*

Quail Track Diagrams, Parts 1, 2 and 4 (TrackMaps)

Signalling Record Society, *Signalling Atlas and Signal Box Directory*

The works of Adrian Vaughan – various publishers

Web Sites

Adrian the Rock's signalling pages – www.roscalen.com/signals

The Signalbox by John Hinson – www.signalbox.org

IngyTheWingy – https://www.flickr.com/people/ingythewingy

Index

Absolute Block (AB)   9, 17, 18, 21, 38, 40, 42, 48, 66, 74, 82, 86, 89, 101, 103, 108, 112–114, 118, 122, 129, 135, 136, 140, 155, 173, 182, 183, 187

Airfix   13, 52, 53

Alstone Crossing   10, 68, 69

Annan   11, 160–163

Annett's Key   70

Appleby North   10, 23, 32, 33

APT   36

ARP   64, 81, 91, 165

Arnside   11, 128–132

Ashton Moss North Junction   10, 88–91

Ashwell   10, 48, 54–56

Askam   11, 128, 137–143

Atherton Goods Yard   10, 79, 83, 84

Axholme Joint Railway   78

Ayr   5, 11, 150, 151, 153, 157, 161, 169, 170

Back light   112, 113

Baguley Fold Junction   10, 88–91

Bala Lake Railway   78

Bamber Bridge Level Crossing Frame   11, 119

Bardon Hill   10, 65, 66

Barrhill   11, 151, 152, 154–158

Barrow-in-Furness   11, 128–130, 133, 134, 136–140, 149

Battlefield Line   67

Bellcrank   169

Bell Code   104, 136, 155, 183

Berth Track Circuit   20

Blackpool North   4, 5, 6, 11, 78, 109–112, 114–119, 137

Blackpool North No. 1   11, 109, 114, 115

Blackpool North No. 2   11, 109, 114–118

Blackrod Junction   10, 79, 87, 88

Blea Moor   10, 23, 27–29

Bolton   5, 10, 79, 83, 87, 88, 92

Bootle   11, 128, 145, 146, 148

Bracket signal   7, 8, 9

Bradford   5, 11, 88, 89, 92, 95, 96, 99, 102, 103, 105, 106

Brierfield Station   11, 119, 123, 124

British Railways (BR)   8, 19, 24, 26, 59, 64, 74, 85, 92, 105, 108, 113, 125, 129, 130, 135, 157, 173, 183

Bromley Cross   10, 79, 87, 88, 119

Burscough Bridge Junction   10, 79, 80

Burton upon Trent   5, 10, 65

Bury Bolton Street   92, 93

Buxton   5, 10, 38, 40, 70, 71, 74, 75

Caledonian Railway   7, 160, 161, 171, 174

Calling on   117, 137

Carleton Crossing   11, 109, 113, 114

Carlisle   5, 10–12, 23–38, 76, 99, 109, 119, 122, 128, 129, 137, 138, 141–146, 148–150, 157, 158, 160–162, 165, 169, 174

Carnforth   11, 23, 26–28, 119, 128–134, 137, 138, 144–146, 148, 149

Castleton East Junction   10, 88, 92–94, 100

Catch Point   32, 54, 60, 102, 112, 165

Caverswall   11, 175–180

CCTV (Closed Circuit TeleVision)   65, 90, 119, 178, 183

Cheltenham Spa   5, 10, 68

Cheshire Lines Committee   12

Chinley Junction   5, 10, 38, 41–43, 70–73

Class 08   64, 71

Class 57   26

Class 60   26, 64, 71, 73, 75

Class 66   27, 28, 33, 44, 64, 66, 71, 73–75, 168

Class 67   64

Class 142   82, 93, 94, 130, 134

Class 150   95, 97, 98, 101, 102, 133, 137, 138, 140

Class 153   180, 182

Class 156   82, 86, 87, 156

Clearing Point   23

Clipstone Junction   58, 60
Crow Nest Junction   10, 79, 82, 83
Culgaith   10, 23, 34, 35
Cutsyke Junction   11, 124, 125

Daisyfield Station   11, 119, 122
Dalton Junction   11, 128, 133–139, 141
DB Schenker   58, 64, 71, 73
Derby   5, 11, 12, 35, 62, 68, 175–180, 182, 183, 185–187
Detection   18, 121, 124, 138, 177
Detonator   8, 34, 109
Direct Rail Services (DRS)   70, 147
Distant Signal   8, 15, 17, 18, 53, 59, 72, 80, 81, 104, 113, 115, 140, 144, 154, 183, 184
DMU (Diesel Multiple Unit)   82, 86, 90, 106, 114, 117, 120, 156, 180
Doll (Dolly)   59, 113, 143, 166
Domino block instrument   108, 109, 113, 135, 139, 183, 187
Drigg   11, 128, 146–148
Dumfries Station   11, 160, 162, 163
Dunragit   11, 151, 157–159

Earle's Sidings   10, 38, 43, 45, 46
East Coast Main Line   13, 18, 21, 53
East Lancashire Railway   78, 88, 92, 96, 97
Edale   10, 38, 42–45, 71
Egginton Junction   11, 175, 185–187
Electric Train Tablet (ETT)   152–154, 156, 157
Elland   11, 99, 107–109
Elmton and Creswell   10, 58–60
English Heritage   9, 102, 122, 141

Facing point lock   8, 19, 22, 67, 103, 134, 135, 138, 139, 153, 172, 178, 179
Fiskerton Junction   9, 13, 15, 16, 18
Fiskerton Station   9, 13, 15–18
Foley Crossing   11, 175–178
Foxfield (Furness Railway)   11, 128, 141–144
Foxfield (Staffordshire)   178
Furness Railway   5, 7, 11, 128, 131, 134, 138, 141, 143, 144, 146–149, 173

Gantry, Gantries   25, 26, 89, 117, 118
Garsdale   10, 23, 29–32
Girvan   11, 151–156, 160
Glasgow   5, 11, 24, 35, 150–152, 158, 160–172, 174
Glasgow and South Western Railway (G&SWR)   5,

7, 11, 24, 84, 150, 151, 160, 165, 171
Glenwhilly   11, 151, 154–158
Grange-over-Sands   11, 128, 131, 132
Great Central Railway   39, 40, 58, 60, 89, 113, 125
Great Northern Railway   21, 48, 105, 106, 181, 185
Great Rocks Junction   10, 71–75, 147
Greetland   11, 99, 103, 105, 107–109
Grindleford   10, 38, 46–48
Ground disc   21, 33, 50, 69, 94, 115, 137, 147–149, 156, 161, 168, 170, 173
Ground frame   13, 16, 29, 49, 86, 153
GSM-R   131
GWR (Great Western Railway)   26, 57, 78, 106, 149

Halifax   11, 99, 104, 105, 107
Hawes Junction   10, 29, 30
Hebden Bridge   11, 96, 99–102, 119, 122
Hellifield South Junction   10, 23–25, 119
Hensall   11, 124, 126, 127
Hickleton   10, 76, 77
Historic Scotland   9
Holywood   11, 160, 164
Home Signal   8, 15, 22, 32–37, 45, 47, 55, 62, 73, 81, 113, 117, 123, 135, 146, 148, 149, 161, 162, 166, 167, 169
Horrocksford Junction   11, 119, 122, 123
Howe and Co.'s Siding   10, 23, 37
HRH Prince Charles   32
Huncoat   11, 120, 121
Hurlford   11, 160, 171

Interim Voice Radio System (IVRS)   176
IFS panel   80, 100, 105, 115
Intermediate Block Section (IBS)   24, 28, 29, 32, 34, 122, 180

Ketton   10, 48–50
Key Token (KT)   9, 74, 85, 86, 147, 149, 152, 158
Kilkerran   11, 150–153
Kilmarnock   157, 160, 169–171, 173, 174
King lever   8, 158, 173
Kirkby (Merseyside)   5, 10, 79, 81, 82, 86, 87
Kirkby Stephen   10, 23, 31, 32
Kirkby Thore   10, 23, 33, 34, 37, 63
Kirkham   11, 109–111

Lancashire and Yorkshire Railway   5, 7, 10, 23, 25, 78–80, 87, 124
Lancashire Derbyshire and East Coast

Railway   60
Langham Junction   10, 48, 53, 54
Lattice post   159, 165, 167, 168, 180
LED (Light Emitting Diode)   36, 50, 69, 161–163, 176
Leeds   5, 10, 12, 23–25, 29, 31, 32, 34–36, 75–78, 89–91, 99, 101, 106, 124, 125, 160
Leicester   5, 10, 12, 40, 48, 57, 61, 65–68, 75, 160
Leicester and Swannington Railway   65, 66
Lincoln   5, 9, 12–14, 19, 21–23
Little Salkeld   35
London and North Eastern Railway (LNER)   12, 13, 20, 37, 84, 89, 105, 107, 109
London and North Western Railway (LNWR)   6, 12, 38–40, 57, 67, 71, 74, 79, 82, 85, 86, 88, 89, 113, 128, 129, 142, 149
London Midland Region   19, 31, 45, 47, 63, 64, 92, 96, 110, 115, 131
Low House Crossing   10, 23, 35, 36
Lowdham   9, 13, 14, 123
Lower Quadrant   18
Lugton   11, 84, 152, 158, 160, 161, 171–174

Mackenzie and Holland   108, 176, 181, 183, 184
Manchester   5, 7, 10, 11, 37–46, 71, 78–84, 87–99, 101.102, 104, 107–109
Mantle Lane   10, 65–67
Manton Junction   10, 48, 50, 51
Mauchline 11, 160, 167–170
Melton Mowbray Station   10, 48, 56, 57
Midge Hall 10, 79, 86, 109, 119
Midland Railway   5, 7, 912–14, 17, 18, 20, 22–30, 38, 40, 41, 43, 45, 48, 53, 54, 56, 58, 61, 62, 67, 68, 70, 75, 78, 105, 124, 125, 128–130, 150, 160, 187
Midland and Great Northern Joint Railway   48
Mill Lane Junction   11, 99, 106
Millom   11, 128, 141–145
Milner Royd Junction   11, 99, 101–105
Moira West Junction   10, 65, 67, 68
Moorthorpe   10, 76
Morton Crossing ground frame   16

National Railway Museum (NRM)   26, 78, 125
Network Rail   8, 9, 15, 18, 31, 34, 63, 65, 68, 70, 116, 122, 126, 135, 148, 153, 156, 168, 178, 184
New Cumnock   11, 160, 167, 168
New Mills Central   10, 38, 40, 41
New Mills South Junction   10, 38, 40–42, 71
Newark Castle   9, 13, 20, 21

No Signaller Key Token (NSKT)   9, 86, 169, 170
North Eastern Railway   12, 20, 29, 37, 78, 125
North Eastern Region   107, 125
North Norfolk Railway   48
North Staffordshire Railway (NSR)   5, 7, 11, 175–177, 180–182, 184–187
North Yorkshire Moors Railway   118
Nottingham   5, 9, 10, 12–23, 25, 51, 58, 65, 75, 160
Nx Panel   51, 67

Oakham Level Crossing   10, 48, 52
Oddingley   10, 68, 70
Oldham   5, 10, 11, 88, 90, 92, 95–98
Oldham Mumps   11, 88, 96–98
One Control Switch (OCS)   38
One Train Staff (OTS)   69, 85
One Train Working (OTW)   111, 124, 158

Parbold   10, 79–82, 121
Park South 11, 128, 134–142, 173
Peak Forest South   10, 42, 43, 71–75
Peterborough   5, 10, 48, 51, 58
Pinxton   10, 58, 61, 62
Poulton-le-Fylde 11, 109–112
Preston   5, 10, 11, 79, 80, 85–87, 109–111, 113, 115, 118–122, 124, 128, 129
Prince of Wales Colliery   11, 124–126

Railway Accident   25, 30, 35
Railway Accident Investigation Branch   7
Rainford Junction   10, 79, 81, 82, 86
Rochdale   10, 88, 93–97, 99–101, 122
Rolleston Crossing   9, 13, 18
Romiley Junction   10, 38.39, 88, 91
Route indicator   115–117, 137
Rufford   10, 79, 85

St. Bees   11, 128, 129, 147–149
Salwick   11, 109, 110
Saxby & Farmer   80, 122, 154
Scotchblock   52
Scropton   11, 175, 181–184
Sellafield   11, 128, 129, 134, 136, 147–149
Settle Junction   10, 23, 27, 28, 128–130
Settle to Carlisle   5, 10, 23, 24
Shaw Station   11, 88, 96, 97
Sheffield   5, 7, 10, 12, 37, 38, 40–48, 71, 75, 76, 124, 160
Shirebrook Junction   10, 58–61, 65

Sighting   18, 36, 45, 58, 73, 113, 133, 149, 151, 167, 186

Silecroft   11, 128, 144–146

Single Line   9, 70, 74, 75, 84–87, 102, 109, 137–140, 147, 148, 152, 157–159, 162, 171–173

Sleight's Sidings East   10, 58, 62

Slotting   18

Smithy Bridge   11, 95, 99–101, 119

Sneinton Crossing Shunt Frame   10, 58, 64, 65

Somerset and Dorset Joint Railway   12

SPAD (Signal Passed at Danger)   35

Stamford Station   10, 48, 49

Stanton Gate Shunt Frame   10, 58, 63

Staythorpe Crossing   9, 13, 18–21

Stencil box   4, 116

Stranraer Harbour   5, 11, 151, 158–160

Stoke on Trent   5, 11, 175–178, 182, 185, 186

Sudbury   11, 175, 180, 181, 183

Swinderby   9, 13, 21–23

Syston   5, 10, 48, 50, 55, 57

TEW   51

Thornhill   11, 160, 164, 165

Tokenless Block (TB)   9, 137–140, 152, 171–173

Totley Tunnel East   10, 38, 47, 48

Toton   12, 58, 61, 63, 64

Towneley   11, 121, 122

Track circuit   9, 30, 33, 39, 41–43, 55, 90, 93, 94, 102, 104, 106, 108, 111, 112, 115, 117, 123, 136, 140, 151, 163, 173, 176, 177, 179, 183, 184, 186, 187

Track Circuit Block (TCB)   9, 21, 34, 38, 40, 48, 65, 66, 78, 82, 83, 97, 100, 101, 108, 109, 111, 122, 128, 129, 176, 187

Trailing point   179

Train Out of Section   136, 173, 182, 183

Train Register   104

Trap Point   54, 72, 112, 149, 156, 161, 165, 168, 173, 174

Train Protection and Warning System (TPWS)   95, 135

TRUST computer   104

Tutbury Crossing   11, 175, 184, 185

Tyer's tablet   154–156

Uffington and Barnack   10, 48, 49

Ulverston   11, 128, 132–134, 136

Uninterruptible Power Supplies (UPS)   104

Upper quadrant   18

Uttoxeter   11, 175, 178–180

Virgin Pendolino   36

Vitriol Works   10, 88, 91, 92

Walkden   10, 79, 84

Welwyn Release   104, 109, 135

Wensleydale Railway   29

Western Region   2,

Whissendine   10, 48, 56

Wicket gate   8, 88, 164, 182, 184

Wigan Wallgate   5, 10, 79, 81–84, 86, 87, 92

Worksop   5, 10, 58, 59

World War I   7, 124, 136, 161

World War II   19, 21, 56, 68, 81, 91, 106, 107, 136, 146, 165

Yardley   100, 102